Suddenly We Didn't Want To Die

Pvt. Elton E. Mackin, USMC, in 1919.

Suddenly We Didn't Want To Die

Memoirs of a World War I Marine

Elton E. Mackin

with an introduction and annotation by
George B. Clark

Foreword by
Lt. Gen. Victor H. Krulak, USMC (Ret.)

★
PRESIDIO

Published by Presidio Press
505 B San Marin Drive, Suite 300
Novato, CA 94945-1340

Presidio Press cloth edition published in 1993
This paperbound edition published in 1996

Library of Congress-in-Publication Data

Mackin, Elton E.
   Suddenly we didn't want to die: memoirs of a World War I marine / Elton E. Mackin : with introduction and annotation by George B. Clark : foreword by Victor H. Krulak.
      p.   cm.
   ISBN: 0-89141-593-9 (paperbound)
   ISBN: 0-89141-498-3 (hardbound)
   1. Mackin, Elton E. 2. World War, 1914–1918—Campaigns—Western.
   3. World War, 1914–1918—Personal narratives, American. 4. Marines—United States—Biography. 5. United States. Marin Corps—Biography.
   I. Title.
D530.M34 1993
940.4' 144—dc20   93-10485
                                                        CIP

Typography by ProImage
Printed in the United States of America

Contents

Foreword

It is difficult now to realize how little the lot of the infantry-man changed in the century that separated the battle of Waterloo from World War I. In both eras, the foot soldier's perspective was a fatalistic one. He entered battle with the not unreasonable presumption that he would die at the hands of an antagonist close enough to see face to face.

Only three developments made any significant change in the soldier's life between the day of Field Marshal Wellington and the day of Field Marshal Haig: the breech-loading rifle, the machine gun, and poison gas. And these simply enhanced the lethality of the doughboy's environment. Such technological innovations as the tank and the airplane were but toys in the Great War and had little effect on the life of the rifleman.

The logistics of the foot soldier's world changed even less during the period. Like his predecessors, the doughboy endured the wet and cold, ate unpalatable food irregularly, and, if wounded, was likely to lie in the mud indefinitely.

This is the somber backdrop to Elton Mackin's unusual account of war at its bottommost level. Writing humbly in the third person, neither seeking credit for the triumphs nor assigning blame for error, Mackin sketches a portrait of war from the private soldier's viewpoint rarely equaled for its brilliance of description or simple sincerity.

Mackin and his fellow marines went to war in the brutal meat grinder of Belleau Wood with only the most rudimentary training. They had been taught to shoot, to use the bayonet, to march, and to do as they were told. That was about it. Their life boiled down to a simple reality: Face the enemy and kill him if you can, for if you don't he will kill you.

Armed with these meager combat skills, leavened with a petrifying fear, Mackin plunged into his first encounter with the enemy. He eloquently describes the seemingly harmless sound of machine-gun bullets—a queer *zeep-zeep*, like insects fleeing to the rear"—and the shock of sudden battlefield death: "It was there that little Purcell stumbled and sat down amidst the grain, his face upturned, with the surprised look of a child hurt in play." Mackin's passionate description of his own reaction is written, as always, in the third person: "The dam of false fortification broke down, and he cried, as a soldier cannot cry, but as only a weary and heartsick lad can pour out the last of his boyish tears."

There is no doubt that the demands of discipline are greatest when infantrymen are obliged, for the first time, to attack a resolute enemy or to defend a position against a determined attack. Mackin's account of his personal reaction to this challenge is both eloquent and sincere: "A flush of shame relieved the scared whiteness of his face. It robbed him of what little strength remained. At that moment boyhood lay behind forever and, back of a small mound of earth, a disciplined soldier faced the long slope ahead, determined to do his part."

As readers savor the simple yet eloquent prose, they will perceive Mackin's steady growth in poise, professionalism, and willingness to accept responsibility. It is plain, however, that the author is never far removed from the gnawing fear that assails every soldier, however experienced he may be. Mackin describes himself and his buddies with unerring clarity: "Ours was not a real hardness. We were too young to be truly hard so soon. We became brittle, which differs from hardness in many degrees. We were just too damned young, and under fire too soon."

In the end, Mackin is painfully and philosophically articulate about it all: "We all had Testaments. A loving people back home in God's country issued them to us with many blessings—and sent us out to fight the Germans. They had not cared to see that we had the tools of war. We borrowed most of those. Christians are such charming people."

During his first three brutal weeks in combat, Mackin's world did not extend beyond the authority of his sergeant. This ended one day when, without warning, he was summoned by the sergeant major and offered a job as a battalion runner—an assignment of considerable responsibility and great hazard. As Mackin describes it, "Suicide squad, that's how the fellows spoke of it. A runner didn't have a chance."

But then, he asks, "Could any man who had pride refuse, and let that stern old sergeant major see the coward that is inside us all? Sure, Sergeant, I'll take it." And he did. Mackin joined three other runners, describing their mutual lot as "four aces, runners gambling with death, playing poker in a game where men are the chips."

After Belleau Wood came Soissons, a procession of bloody, wrenching experiences. In one instance Mackin tells of another runner who died after failing to get his job done, then delivers a heart-wrenching epitaph characteristic of the literary heights to which his writing often rises: "Little crosses stand above the dead. They do not tell how men died. They hide the bitter human stories of the war. They seldom stand alone. Men see to that."

Although only modestly educated, Mackin possessed a formidable intellect and ability to express himself—a capacity for weaving pain and suffering into a web of almost paralyzing reality.

Here, for certain, is the natural-born historian, whose simple chronicle rings with the resonance of truth. Mackin's brilliant, almost elegant, treatment of the lot of the private soldier in World War I deserves a special place among the countless volumes written about that tragic conflict.

Victor H. Krulak
Lieutenant General, USMC (Ret.)

Introduction

This is the story of a young marine who fought in the Great War, told in his own words. It could just as easily be the story of any one of the two million men who joined the American Expeditionary Forces (AEF) in France during the years 1917 to 1919. Fortunately for us, Elton E. Mackin was an intelligent man who clearly and concisely set down his thoughts on paper. Mackin also left an oral account of his experiences in tape-recorded interviews with his son in the 1970s. Those tape recordings greatly assisted the editor in developing the annotations that are found in the text of Mackin's book.

Elton Mackin was born 22 February 1898 in Lewiston, New York, a small town just north of Niagara Falls. When he was six weeks old, his father, Arnot Mackin, drowned while helping a friend reach safety after a boating accident. Elton's mother later remarried and had four more children, three of whom were daughters.

Mackin's formal education ended when he graduated from high school in 1917, a noteworthy achievement for a working-class youth in the early twentieth century. Innate intelligence, coupled with a more than adequate dose of common sense and service in the Marine Corps, completed Mackin's informal higher education.

After high school, Mackin worked at various jobs until 23 December 1917, when he enlisted in the marines. He later said that a story in the *Saturday Evening Post* prompted him to do so. No personal record describing his early months as a marine survived, but we can guess that he was well trained for the ultimate role of any marine: "to kill or be killed," as he so often liked to state.

Long before Mackin took the oath of enlistment in his local recruiting office, the Marine Corps, not wanting to be left out of what promised to be the biggest conflict since the Civil War, managed to convince Secretary of War Newton D. Baker that it could supply a regiment of trained infantry as soon as war was declared. The marine commandant, Maj. Gen. George Barnett, soon received assurances that the army, desperate for manpower, would gladly accept a regiment of marines for service in France should the need arise. The army was true to its word: the chosen regiment, the 5th Marines, sailed as part of the first U.S. troop contingent sent over to bolster flagging Allied morale. Unfortunately, Gen. John J. Pershing, commanding the newly created AEF, and his staff were more concerned with building a first-class army, literally from nothing, than they were about a single regiment of marines.

At first, the regiment was brigaded with several army regiments in the 1st Division, a regular army outfit. But, because the army's tables of organization and equipment called for four infantry regiments in a division, not five, the marines were assigned other tasks—mostly construction and labor details. Pershing, facing mounting pressure to give the marines a combat job, decided in late 1917 to pull the regiment from the 1st Division and brigade it with several other army regiments then becoming available.

By February 1918, the 6th Marine Regiment and 6th Machine Gun Battalion had arrived in France and, together with the 5th Marines, combined to form the 4th Brigade (U.S. Marines). Shortly thereafter, the 3d Brigade, made up of two regular army infantry regiments and the 5th Machine Gun Battalion; the 2d Field Artillery Brigade, consisting of the 12th, 15th, and 17th Field Artillery battalions; the 4th Machine Gun Battalion; and the 2d Engineer Regiment were joined by the 4th Brigade to form the 2d Division, which quickly became known as a first-class outfit. Later, many said it was the best division in France, challenged only by the 1st Division.

The marines fit in well, becoming more and more like soldiers in appearance, if not in name. Because they were supplied from the same stores used to keep army units operating, the marines were forced to replace their trademark forest green uniforms with army khaki as the greens wore out. To avoid being confused with doughboys, the marines carefully transferred buttons and emblems featuring the Marine Corps's distinctive globe, eagle, and anchor to their new tunics, caps, and helmets.

In the middle of March 1918, the 2d Division entered the lines in the Toul sector. The sight of their first casualties convinced the division's doughboys and marines that they were in a real war, indeed. In mid-May they moved to an area slightly south and west of Bar-le-Duc and Vitry-le-François. During this period the 4th Brigade lost its commander, Brig. Gen. Charles Doyen, who was succeeded by army Brig. Gen. James G. Harbord. It was an interesting phenomenon: a marine officer replaced by a soldier. But the marines took it well and never gave Harbord anything less than their complete loyalty. The reaction to their new commander is best illustrated by the fact that, after the war, the brigade's officers commissioned a portrait of Harbord to be hung in the Army and Navy Club in Washington.

Harbord held his marine counterparts in similar high regard. He knew he was getting command of a crack outfit. The story is told that Pershing called Harbord, then serving as AEF chief of staff, into his office and advised him that he was being given command of "the best brigade in the army, and if it fails I'll know who is to blame."

By the spring of 1918 the war was well into its fourth year. The Germans, realizing that the rapid American buildup would soon tip the scale irrevocably in favor of the Allies, launched a series of massive assaults at various portions of the

Allied line. The Boche moved rapidly westward as the stunned British and French armies gave up ground.

The French high command begged Pershing, who was patiently husbanding his forces until he could field a separate American army, to send them all available AEF units to help stem the German advance in the Aisne-Marne area, where the French army had fought the Boche to a standstill in 1914. This time, however, there were no fresh French troops on hand to work another miracle. Pershing approved the request, offering the French "all that we have." To have done otherwise would have been tantamount to betraying the Allied cause.

The 1st Division was already in the lines in the Montdidier sector and, when the German advance stalled there, the division gave the Boche a bloody nose with an assault on Cantigny on 28 May. Pershing offered the 2d and 3d divisions to the French command and promised to send additional units as fast as they were deemed combat ready.

The 2d Division started along its path to glory on the morning of 31 May 1918, when its troops began boarding French trucks for the trip to Meaux, a village about twenty-five miles east of Paris on the Marne River and some fifteen miles west of the Germans' front-line trace. It was a race against time as the Boche were rapidly rolling westward and the French command was so confused by the situation that it was sending reinforcements all over the map. Leading elements of the 4th Brigade were ordered to dismount at a town named Lizy, a little north and east of Meaux. But the marines were just one of the division's units, which were scattered all over the area. The story of how each unit found its parent and subordinate headquarters would make a chapter in itself. It is enough to say that the division was in a chaotic state and took several days to assemble. There was no divisional artillery and no supply trains, and none became available for more than a week.

Fortunately, the Germans were also in disarray and had

stopped to reorganize in and around the small town of Bouresches, a few miles north and west of Château-Thierry. The Boche especially wanted to take the town of Belleau.

The 3d Division's 7th Machine Gun Battalion was the first unit to arrive in the sector, setting up on the south bank of the Marne across from Château-Thierry. Like a latter-day group of Horatios, the battalion's men bravely held the bridge there as elements of the 2d Division began to arrive and sort themselves out. The result was that the 4th Brigade occupied the northern part of the division's front and the 3d Brigade dug in along the southern half. This meant the brigades' positions were the reverse of those specified in the division's operations order. The confused trip and assembly resulted in chance determining the ground the two brigades finally occupied. No one knew then that Belleau Wood, which lay across open ground in front of the marines' positions and was only a small portion of the Château-Thierry sector, would soon become an important—and ultimately very bloody—segment of that part of the front.

It was there that a rift began to develop between the dough-boys and marines. For security reasons, the AEF refused to allow reporters to identify units by their numerical designations. The restriction did not apply to names, however, and American newspapermen—most notably Floyd Gibbons of the Chicago *Tribune*—identified the 4th Brigade as the "Marine Brigade" in their dispatches from the front. This meant that Americans, hungry for news about what their boys were doing in France, learned that "the marines are fighting at Château-Thierry," or that "the marines have taken Belleau Wood." Needless to say, their army comrades did not appreciate the publicity and loudly complained about "those damned head-line-grabbing sonofabitching gyrenes," adding a few unprintable expletives for good measure.

The 2d Division infantry units arriving in that sector encountered French troops crying *"la guerre est fini."* One French major ordered a marine captain, Lloyd Williams, to fall back. Williams's response became a Marine Corps battle cry: "Retreat? Hell! We just got here!" He then ordered his platoon leaders to take up firing positions and "let the 'Frogs' pass through." Next, Williams penned a message to Lt. Col. Frederick M. Wise, his battalion commander, which read:

> The French major gave Captain Corbin written orders to fall back . . . I have countermanded the order . . . kindly see that the French do not shorten their artillery range . . . 82d and 84th companies are on their way to fill the gap on the right of this company.

The first few days of the continued German assault during early June were most murderous for the Boche as the 2d Division's doughboys and marines took careful aim and shot down the enemy in windrows as they crossed the wheat fields. Sustained, well-aimed rifle fire will stop any army, no matter how good that army is. Flesh and blood can stand just so much before even the most courageous soldier gives way. What happened, of course, was that the Germans took up defensive positions and then it was the Marine Brigade's turn to make inroads in all the nooks and crannies the enemy occupied—and Belleau Wood was loaded with them.

Belleau Wood, known to the French as the *Bois de Belleau,* was later renamed the *Bois de la Brigade de Marines* after it was strewn with their bodies. Early on the morning of 6 June 1918, after receiving orders from the French Sixth Army to launch an attack, the 1st Battalion, 5th Marines advanced from its positions, moving northward toward the towns of Torcy and Bussiares. The marines took their initial objective, Hill 142, but the battalion was so badly shot up that Maj. Julius S. Turrill ordered his men to halt along the ridge and dig in.

The French, meanwhile, ordered the Marine Brigade to take Belleau Wood and Bouresches, which lay just beyond it.

General Harbord ordered the 3d Battalion, 5th Marines and the 3d Battalion, 6th Marines to assault the woods just after noon, but German machine gunners were ready and cut both battalions to shreds. Now *two* battalions from the 5th Marines had been decimated. The 3d Battalion, 6th Marines was also badly mauled, but not to the same devastating extent. It was one of the bloodiest days of the entire war for the Americans, and many veterans of the "Old Corps" were lost, a fact that would change the complexion and character of the Marine Corps forever. It would mainly be replacements who would carry the fight to the Boche, and their replacements after them, and so on until the woods was finally won.

Elton Mackin, or "Slim" as he calls himself in the book, was assigned to the 138th Company, 3d Replacement Battalion when he arrived in the sector on 7 June. He describes himself as having been as green as any "boot marine" could be. He missed the fighting on 6 June, and his taped conversations suggest that he always felt a sense of guilt because of that.

Mackin and his fellow marines spent the balance of the month fighting to take Belleau Wood. The dominant local terrain feature, but measuring only one square mile in area, it naturally loomed large in everyone's minds. But the fighting took place over a much wider sector, and the battalion Mackin joined, the 1st Battalion, 5th Marines, continued to occupy the ground it had taken on the first bloody day of the battle. Like the rest of the brigade and division, Mackin's outfit was actively engaged the entire time—except for a brief respite when the brigade was relieved by the 7th Infantry Regiment. By the end of June, the marines had driven out the Germans and controlled all of Belleau Wood.

The 2d Division was withdrawn from the line for a much needed rest, but soon found itself caught up in the action again in mid-July when the French command ordered the division north toward Soissons. Another bloody assault was in the offing for the division, which was quickly growing accustomed to its role as a "fire brigade" for the Allied command.

Mackin was by then a full-fledged member of the 67th Company, although he many times refers to his status as being that of a "damn replacement." Regular marines at the time—and probably to this day—did not accept anyone into their clan who hadn't suffered through the worst times with them.

During the brief rest period following the bitter struggle for Belleau Wood, General Harbord received a second star and replaced Maj. Gen. Omar Bundy as division commander. While Col. Wendell Neville, commander of the 6th Marines, was in the hospital during the interim, his temporary replacement, Lt. Col. Harry Lee, assumed command of the Marine Brigade. Neville returned just in time to take over the brigade before the Aisne-Marne (Soissons) offensive.

Mackin relates how much pressure was put on the division, especially its foot soldiers, to arrive at the attack position immediately—if not sooner. The exhausted infantry of both brigades marched northward to the Soissons salient, arriving at Villers-Cotterêts Forest late on 17 July. They were ordered to get into position quickly and prepare to lead the assault the next day. John W. Thomason, in his colorful book *Fix Bayonets,* describes the agonies of that forced march and assembly in a chapter titled "The Charge at Soissons." From Private Mackin's perspective, however, it all seemed very confusing.

But the 2d Division arrived in time and, on 18 July, the 5th Marines led the assault on the division's left wing. It was an attack conducted with minimal planning and, for the most part, caught a surprised foe relatively unprepared. It was no cakewalk, but it wasn't nearly as bad as Belleau Wood had been for the regiment. The following day, however, resistance stiffened, and the 6th Marines, who led off that morning, got clobbered. Mackin's description of his own hectic day on the eighteenth features some of the best writing in his book.

* * *

The 2d Division was withdrawn from the front for the next few weeks. Brigadier General John A. Lejeune, USMC, replaced Harbord as the division commander on 25 July as the division reassembled about thirty miles northeast of Paris. Then, by stages, the division transferred to an area near Nancy, where, after a few days' rest, it was assigned to the relatively quiet Pont-à-Mousson sector. The division remained there until it was called to join the recently formed U.S. First Army for a planned attack on the Saint-Mihiel salient. By 20 August, division units were gathered in the vicinity of Colombey-les-Belles, a town about fifteen miles south of Toul.

The 2d Division took up positions on the southern face of the salient, where the First Army stood poised for the assault. The division was on I Corps's left flank, tucked in closely to the 89th Division on IV Corps's right. The attack commenced early on 12 September, with the 3d Brigade leading and the Marine Brigade following in support. The 5th Marines trailed the 9th Infantry on the right flank and the 6th Marines moved behind the 23d Infantry on the division's left. Although several divisions had their work cut out for them that day, the 2d had a reasonably good day compared with its experiences on previous and later occasions.

The Marine Brigade took over the lead the next day and set out to drive the Boche from their outposts. But the Germans had long before recognized the weakness of the salient and withdrew after offering little more than face-saving resistance. The 2d Division's losses were minimal during the two days in which it was actively engaged at Saint-Mihiel.

The division then returned to French control, this time as part of Gen. Henri Gouraud's Fourth Army, from 27 September through 10 October. During this period, General Gouraud ordered Major General Lejeune to take the formidable German positions on Blanc-Mont ridge. Lejeune agreed to carry out the assault even though he knew the French had failed with heavy losses in several desperate attempts.

On 3 October, following an awesome artillery barrage, the Marine Brigade moved out on the 2d Division's left, with the 3d Brigade on the right and French light tanks supporting both wings. The marines and doughboys advanced steadily up the slopes of the ridge, making considerable progress before the day was over. The following day the Boche were better prepared, however, and the 5th Marine Regiment was virtually wiped out.

Survivors of the slaughter say it was the bloodiest action they ever saw. Private Mackin was awarded the Distinguished Service Cross and two Silver Star citations by the army, and later received the Navy Cross for his valor as a battalion runner from 3–5 October. Mackin says several times in taped conversations that he was sure he would die, so why should he try to prevent it? His daughter Marie later said he told her that his subsequent disability caused by "shell shock" was the result of the terrible shelling to which he was constantly exposed on the fourth.

At least one battalion from the 5th Marines was almost routed on 4 October. Mackin's commander, Maj. George Hamilton, one of the unsung heroes of the war, managed— with the help of several officers and enlisted men, including Mackin—to extricate the 1st Battalion from a position of certain destruction as it was being encircled by German artillery and machine-gun fire.

After preventing the potential rout, Hamilton led his men forward, still under terrible fire, and captured the enemy position. Their losses were monstrous, reducing the battalion to less than company strength.

On the night of 6–7 October, the untried 36th Division, a National Guard outfit from Texas and Oklahoma, began relieving badly mauled 2d Division elements and four days later took over the entire sector. The Guardsmen suffered, too, but the Boche had been handled so roughly by the 2d Division that they could do no more than try to hold the ground they stood on.

The 2d Division returned to U.S. First Army control on 25 October and marched to Landres-et-Saint-Georges, arriving the night of 30–31 October and relieving the 42d "Rainbow" Division. Early the next morning a massive artillery barrage signaled the start of the final battle of the war for the Americans. Although the division advanced as planned, the French and American units on its flanks were tardy. Even with both flanks in the air, the division managed to seize its objectives. The next night, the two army infantry regiments, supported by a battalion from the 5th Marines, advanced four miles in total darkness and foul weather, nearly capturing a German division commander and his staff.

The Allies continued to advance against an adversary on the verge of collapse. Finally, the distraught enemy agreed to terms for an armistice to take effect at 11:00 A.M. on 11 November. That fact had little impact on the men in Mackin's outfit, however, as engineers from the 89th Division successfully spanned the Meuse River with pontoon bridges on the night of 10–11 November and two battalions of the 5th Marines, including Mackin's, crossed over against fierce resistance to prepare for an assault on Sedan that never came.

With the war over, the 2d Division was selected to occupy part of the Rhineland until a peace accord could be finalized. Mackin's story does not include the occupation period, although he remained in Germany until May 1919. He returned to his hometown that same month, after being honorably discharged from the Marine Corps.

Although his records do not reflect any combat wounds, Mackin talks in his taped conversations about being tagged for medical evacuation three times. Each time, however, he tore up the tag and remained with his company. He mentions it matter-of-factly, with no apparent attempt to impress the listener. He described being hit in the back by a bullet or shell fragment on one of those occasions, leaving him temporarily paralyzed from the waist down. Later, when he found he could move his toes, he left the casualty collection point and "went home" to his company, receiving no official recognition of his wounds.

As noted earlier, Mackin suffered from shell shock, a malady common to soldiers in the Great War. The pension he was later awarded as a result of this condition was the culmination of many years of negotiation with the Veterans Administration.

After returning home from the war, Mackin found employment first with the Niagara Mohawk Power Company, then as a clerk with the Pennsylvania Railroad. In 1921 he married Emily M. Goodsite, a young lady he met at a dance in Canton, Ohio. The newlyweds returned to Lewiston, where Mackin became a town constable. Their first child, Wallace, was born nearly four years later, and shortly thereafter Mackin and his family headed for Florida and a new life.

Mackin's children said one of their earliest memories was of their father working on his memoir in the early 1930s. They said he continued to write and revise the manuscript until late in his life. After Mackin's death, they found several onionskin carbon copies amongst his personal effects. The copies reflect a number of changes Mackin made as the work went through a steady evolution into what the reader finds in this volume.

The Great Depression forced the Mackins back to Milan, Ohio, where they lived with his widowed father-in-law. Like many men at that time, Mackin worked as a laborer on Public Works Administration projects. He also joined the local Veterans of Foreign Wars post when it became active, and not long afterward joined the American Legion. His personality and energy led him to become a post commander in both organizations. Mackin's subsequent appointment as an employment officer at a new Veterans Administration office no doubt contributed to his popularity in the veterans' community.

The Mackin family moved again in 1935, this time to Norwalk, Ohio. Unfortunately, Mackin was associated with

12

the losing political party in the 1936 elections and so lost his job with the VA. Not long after that, he went to work for the Lake Shore Electric Railway, but it went out of business in late 1937; again he was unemployed. Mackin subsequently found temporary jobs as a freight handler and appliance salesman before being hired as a clerk for the local Selective Service draft board in 1939.

When World War II ended, Mackin and his son started an appliance store in Norwalk that survived until 1957. In his later years, Mackin worked as a bus driver for handicapped and retarded children, and as a custodian at the local county office building. He and his wife also took in foster children. The couple remained in Norwalk after Mackin retired. He died on 21 February 1974, one day shy of his seventy-sixth birthday.

George B. Clark

PART I

June, Belleau Wood

"Hey, Pop!"

Zero hour. Dawn of 6 June 1918. Hushed commands brought the chilled, sleepy men to their feet. A skirmish line formed along the edge of the woods. There were last-minute instructions and bits of advice flung here and there. Careless of cover, the men in the first wave stood about in the wheat, adjusting belts and hitching combat packs to easier positions. The early morning mist thinned under the warmth of a red-balled sun. There were half-heard murmurs of conversation among the men and, at times, a spurt of nervous laughter, quickly stilled. The entire front was quiet where we were. There was only the distant sound of far-off guns warning the lines to come awake.

First Sergeant "Pop" Hunter,[1] the 67th Company's top-cutter, strode out into the field and, a soldier to the last, threw a competent glance to right and left, noting the dress of his company line. Pop was an old man, not only of portly figure and graying hair but in actual years, for more than thirty years of service lay behind him.

No bugles. No wild yells. His whistle sounded shrilly. Once. His cane swung overhead and forward, pointing toward the first objective, a thousand yards of wheat away: the tensely quiet edge of German-held Belleau Wood.

The spell was broken. A single burst of shrapnel came to

---

1. Daniel A. Hunter of Westerly, Rhode Island, killed in action (KIA) 6 June 1918.

greet the moving line of men. There was a scream of pain, a plaintive cry of hurt. In some alarm, a soldier yelled, "Hey, Pop, there's a man hit over here!"

Pop's reply was terse and pungent: "C'mon, goddamnit! He ain't the last man who's gonna be hit today."

We Were Young

We met the war at a crossroad. We were young. Europe had been aflame for more than three years, and we had come a goodly way to smell its smoke. Full of wonderings and wanderings, full of restlessness and spice, we heard the war scream and writhe and crash among the distant trees. The guns around us added to the din, and suddenly we didn't want to die.

The fellows walked with disciplined eyes that stared in fascination. They walked in fear and pride. They shot quick glances here and there at other men to gather strength, to imitate their still-faced calm, and to match their stride. It was difficult to still that awful growing dread. Dark of night would have been welcome then, so that a man might hide the terror in his eyes. The glare of sunlit day was hard to face with other fellows watching all your thoughts.

We met our war at a crossroad. We were young. We didn't know then that we could be old in such a brief time, nor that a short way beyond we would turn a page on boyhood's span and carry scars ever after down life's roads.

The war met us at a crossroad near Marigny Château. Because the long-range German guns over Torcy way were spewing bits of hate in the form of high explosives, we were put into the partial shelter of the roadside hedge, allowing time to pass. The war had come down our road to meet us. We took the time to study it, to note its greeting. We had an hour or more of sunny June-time afternoon through which to wait and watch and gather swift impressions.

Somewhere off to the north of us, a German battery was zeroed in, firing from the depths of Belleau Wood. The shells

19

came down in perfect flights of four, always of four, and four, and four, with just enough space between blasts for the crews to serve the guns. Methodical, precise, deadly, the gunfire swept the crossing. Men and horses died. Huge old army camions and Thomas trucks crashed and smashed and burned; engineers died while recklessly moving the wrecks to keep the roadway clear.

Have you ever watched a gut-shot horse, screaming, drag his shell-killed mate, his dead driver, and his wagon down a bit of road until he dies? Horses die more noisily than men, as a rule. Most men die quietly if death comes soon. They seldom make a lot of fuss—unless the first dulling shock has worn away and pain begins to run in searing waves. Even the strongest weaken and scream, given enough of burning pain.

The business of war is a pressing one and movement must go on in spite of anything. We were enthralled. We were privileged men to lie out there, short rifle range from carnage, learning, watching how things went.

Traffic on the roadway scarcely slowed. Horse teams went their way, their heads held high, snorting as they passed insensate things. We hadn't thought 'til then of men who prayed through those awful yards of hell and crashing death.

A figure came among us along the right of way, seeking our lieutenant in command.[1] Word spread among us that a runner had come down to guide us in. We would be needed on the firing line that night.

---

1. The officer referred to was probably 1st Lt. Felix M. Beauchamp, who would earn the Distinguished Service Cross and later the Navy Cross for his actions at Blanc-Mont on 3–4 October 1918. Mackin was part of the 3d Replacement Battalion, 138th Company, which reached Hill 142 on the evening of 7 June 1918. The 67th Company's muster rolls indicate that Mackin didn't arrive until 9 June, but other documentation makes it quite clear that he joined the unit on the seventh. Men were not always put on the muster roll the

We had heard tales about the runners—the risks they took, the price they paid. Not without reason were they included among the elite details that formed the "suicide squad." We understood that the work, except in an emergency, was voluntary, and that no man need accept the job as a regular assignment if he preferred otherwise. Of all the risks we had heard about along the front, we were of one mind concerning the job those fellows did. "No runner job for us—too dangerous."[1]

A wounded fellow, walking, came our way and was hailed with a shower of eager questions by us "boots." He didn't even take the time to talk to us, just passed us by, stony-faced, looking holes through us in contempt, as though he had a quality we lacked and didn't think us much.

We heard him call the runner Jack,[2] saw him stop to chat awhile, and, later, answer our lieutenant civilly enough.

As the wounded man left us, drifting back to find an ambulance, he shouted, "Hey, Jack, has the outfit got to hold the woods with them goddamn replacements?"

We didn't know how young and scared we were, nor how much we showed it. Some of us were to know the runner, Jack, and soldier with him for many miles and in many places.

---

day they arrived, but were left on their replacement company muster roll instead. Company clerks didn't always have time to fill in the forms—they too were very busy as riflemen.

1. Mackin, in a 1973 taped interview, stated that he decided to become a runner because a man was allowed some freedom of action and, even though it was very dangerous, he could take care of himself rather than leaving that to someone else.

2. Sergeant John M. Fackey, who received two Silver Star citations and the croix de guerre.

Sign Post

The path out of Lucy-le-Bocage skirted a trampled garden, passed a dead cow, followed the road to a gap in the hedge, and dropped into a drainage ditch. It cornered a bit of the field, and was covered, at least to our minds, by the promise offered by a copse of saplings across some open ground.

At the copse, the path divided, one way going forward toward the ravine, the other turning half-left through the underbrush to Hill 142. A German soldier had died in the fork of the path, grotesquely and in pain. One upflung arm, spread-fingered and beseeching, was caught among the branches of a scrubby bush.

For the guidance of travelers, some humorous soul had laced a cardboard sign between the dead man's fingers. Rough lettering spelled out the words "Battalion P.C." above an arrow pointing west.

Initiation

The garish flare of a star shell blasting the deep gloom brought into relief a file of replacements cautiously groping their way along the front opposite Torcy, and gave to each his first view of no-man's-land at night.

The blinding light froze every man in his tracks. Rigid, their figures merged with the shadows of the wood so that no enemy eye might detect movement among them. These green troops had been making their way toward the firing line since early dark. Now, with night half gone, they were filtering through the trees along the crest of a ridge to take positions in that thin line of shallow trenches and foxholes which constituted the only barrier between Paris and the German drive.

"Come on, close up! Close up!" came the hoarse whisper of a guide. The ghastly light waned and suddenly went out. The muted sound of movement came from the head of the column. Men dared to breathe freely again. Stiffened fingers relaxed their startled grip on rifle stocks, and again the men groped forward.

After a few hundred yards came a command: "Pass the word to halt!" Each received the whispered message as he bumped into the man ahead and soon the diminishing sound of rasping branches and stumbling feet ceased entirely. Shortly, there came a vague activity from the rear of the column and a gradual shuffling forward of a few steps at a time, interspersed with whispered pleas to "Step out a little!" or "Hold it!"

Shadowy forms wandered from man to man. A quiet voice of authority bade each: "Take a five-pace interval and lie down!"

One felt an oppressive loneliness at losing contact with the next in line, a feeling soon replaced by one of relief as tired bodies relaxed on cool earth. The occasional boom of a heavy gun gave background to the eerie, brooding gloom. Somewhere a machine gun rapped its message into the darkness. At times, the sharp crack of a rifle in the hands of a nervous watcher punctuated the stillness. The damned replacements had arrived.

Slim lay for a time with his head pillowed on folded arms. He needed sleep, but the numbing physical exhaustion which had been draining his vitality for hours was suddenly replaced by the torture of outraged nerves. Through his thoughts raced the crowding incidents of three hectic days.

It seemed an age since the evening that had brought sudden orders to entrain for the front. He had a confused memory of forced marches, of a long ride in boxcars jammed with others of his kind. Passenger trains had been shunted aside to let their troop train through; the cheering populations of the little towns of France had turned out along the way. He had also caught a glimpse of Paris from the railroad yards, where sentries had stood at car doors while late afternoon had faded into dusk—at which time the ride to the north could be resumed in comparative safety from aerial observation.

Then Meaux, in a sprinkling rain, and a few hours of rest in sodden blankets along an avenue of great trees, while the sky to the north was lighted by a never-ending cannonade whose distant roar and tremble penetrated even to the back areas of the Zone of Advance.

Morning. War waited 'til then to show its awful face. Refugees in endless streams followed the ditches or clung to the roads with pitiful belongings piled high on ancient barrows. Great two-wheeled farm carts, stacked with the possessions of hurried departures, were here and there crowned with little children, singly or in groups of two and three, tucked amid the jumble of featherbeds, poultry coops, and sacks of forage. In all that pitiful column not one laughed, nor paused to greet the "*soldats*" as the French are wont to do. They

24

picked their way to the west—hopeless, fear-stricken, heart-sick, and weary, but such is war.

Breasting that stream as best it could in broken formation, Slim's column had taken up its march toward the muttering guns beyond the horizon.

Around a great bend in the road had come a cavalcade of Ford ambulances carrying shattered fragments of battle to the rear. At the sight of the green-clad marine column a cheer of frenzied exhortation had risen from the lesser wounded who rode seat, running board, and tailgate.

"Gyrenes, gyrenes, you—you goddamn leathernecks, go take 'em!"

"You're needed up there, bad. The outfit is all shot to hell—go get 'em, marines!"

Cries and curses; loving curses from the lips of broken but unbeaten men. Their feverish exhortations were an inspiration, a challenge, a comrade's benediction, almost a prayer.

Then had come a train of trucks into which the marines had been crowded like sheep—the sheep in those cattle cars going through the Pennsy yards back home, headed for Hares Island and slaughter.

Another march. As night closed in they began to pass scattered batteries of barking 75s. Then single file over dim trails that wound through wood and field, drawing ever nearer to the distant rattle of "sho-shos"[1] and rifle fire.

In one such field they'd heard a queer *zeep-zeep*, like insects fleeing to the rear. Occasionally, something cracked while passing close at hand, and Slim felt a thrill of terror upon hearing a knowing voice say, "Machine guns, double

---

1. Chauchat, a French automatic rifle. This replaced the marines' favorite weapon, the Lewis gun, with which they had been equipped in the United States. It was never as satisfactory or beloved as the Lewis gun.

time!" They ran into a war-torn village, where shells had slammed through tile roofs and moved whole walls of houses into streets to pile the broken rubble in smoking, dusty heaps.

Their route led them through a hedge and into a field of wheat where again the zip of bullets from some unseen gun had loaned wings to their feet as they dashed for the looming shelter of friendly trees.

It was there that little Purcell had stumbled and sat down amidst the grain.[1] His upturned face had greeted Slim with the surprised look of a child hurt in play. Even as he stopped to lend a hand, Purcell's boyish figure had begun to settle back and an uplifted hand had suddenly gone limp upon Slim's arm. In sudden awe he realized he was witness to the passing of a boy who had won the love of older comrades and whose voice had often joined with his in singing away the miles.

Slim had left him as he lay, carrying only the memory of a childish face—strangely at peace—looking up into the clear, cold light of summer stars.

He stumbled on to rejoin the column. The habit of discipline is strong, and the trained soldier may answer subconsciously to the call of duty though his heart may pause for a time at the altar of a friend's sacrifice.

The night had grown quieter. Slim lay still while his thoughts seethed with the confusion of past hours. Even the normal noises of a quiet front-line night passed unnoticed. It was as though his whole being was in tune with the distant rolling cadence of the guns.

How long he lay there inert he did not know—nor care. Repeated pictures of Purcell, laughing, questioning, and now

---

1. The name Purcell does not show up on the muster roll for June 1918, nor was anyone by that name KIA during the period. Mackin apparently changed a few names for personal reasons. Several more pseudonyms appear later in the text but have not been identified as such.

dead, weakened his resistance until a dry sob, which would not be denied, at last wrung itself free. The dam of his false fortitude broke down and he cried—as a soldier cannot cry, but as only a weary heartsick lad can pour out the last of his boyish tears in facing that change which is the boundary between childhood and bitter reality.

That was how Sergeant McCabe found him.[1] A rough hand clutched his shoulder and snatched him back to the threshold of war. "It's too late to snivel now, Bud, so grab that tool and start digging." The noncom's voice was full of the contempt of the professional soldier for the amateur.

Slim wanted to explain that it was more grief than fear to which he had surrendered, and he even managed a word about Purcell, but the manner in which McCabe answered showed that Slim's tears had branded him a weakling; he fell silent before the searing sarcasm of his superior.

"Hell, Bud, you'd think you were the only guy in this man's war to lose a pal. We've all lost 'em up here, an' we want *men* in their places—not babies! Now, dig in!"

As Slim set to work, he took time to look about him. The gray of approaching dawn had begun to dim the black shadows of the night. The stars still showed, but their brilliance had paled before the first flush of morning. He found himself just within the fringe of trees that crested a low ridge, facing a long, gradual slope of standing wheat on which the mist lay like a blanket.

It was from out there that the star shell had cast its ghostly light, but a while before and, with a start, Slim realized that somewhere beyond that field was the enemy he had come to meet in battle. Suddenly mindful of his lack of shelter, he hurried to dig a rifle pit, piling the loose earth at the end of his grave-like excavation facing the edge of the wood.

---

1. Sergeant John C. McCabe, KIA 4 October 1918.

The increasing light exposed an irregular line of men similarly engaged, and the feverish manner in which they worked bespoke knowledge of a danger that lurked beyond the mist. Tough roots resisted the shovel and the delay thus occasioned spurred the boy to a frenzy of effort. In his heart was the fear that he wouldn't be well under cover before daylight revealed him to the eye of a sniper. It seemed his mound would not take form at a rate fast enough to match the approaching dawn.

A distant gun barked and immediately after its muffled report came a screaming roar followed by a flash—an explosion. There was a spatter of falling fragments among the trees; somewhere near at hand, an anguished voice cried out in pain. As though by signal, entire batteries took up the chorus. The clatter of a machine gun joined in, then another, as the rising tide of sound merged into a crescendo that stifled thought and, for a moment, paralyzed all motion. Shrapnel rained upon the ridge. A running figure dashed along the line, yelling for everyone to take cover. Men sought shelter behind half-finished mounds of earth and hugged the ground. Whole trees crashed down as heavy shells shook and jarred the earth. Fumes from the explosions became a blanket that crept over the forest floor like a pall. There were cries for "First aid, first aid!" Other cries—wordless, terrible cries—told of men in agony.

Figures moved among the inexperienced men. One of them crouched at Slim's side and he heard the voice of Sergeant McCabe yelling in his ear, "Fix bayonets! Fix bayonets, an' watch that goddamn wheat!"

"Are they coming?" Slim managed to croak from a throat that seemed to choke the words in his breast.

"Yeah, when this barrage lifts, they'll come—and in numbers, Bud. Shoot low and be ready to go meet them if they get too close."

The import of the noncom's words penetrated Slim's consciousness like a sentence of doom. Further speech was beyond him. The prospect of using a bayonet, of facing enemy bayonets in action, was his pet horror. The very thought left him weak.

"Don't turn yellow and try to run," McCabe shouted. "If you do and the Germans don't kill you, I will." With that he left.

Fascinated, Slim watched the sergeant progress down the line. He marveled that anyone could walk through such a hail of steel, expecting with every step to see the man go down.

As McCabe passed from sight among the trees, the meaning of his last words suddenly came to Slim. A flush of shame chased the scared whiteness from his face and for a moment he lay his head upon his arm. He felt robbed of what little strength remained. To be thought a coward on his first day of battle, in his first hour of action, threatened to place him beyond the regard of these men he strove so hard to copy.

The taunt had reached him and hurt his pride. At that moment, boyhood lay forever behind, a page of life's story had turned. In back of a small mound of earth, a disciplined soldier faced the long slope ahead, determined to do his part.

The shell fire slackened. Bursts were falling behind the ridge now, centered on support positions, sweeping favored paths and roads over which reserves might come. How well the old Boche knew this bit of front! Just two days back he had consolidated here, and now his dead and the debris of battle lay about. The ridge had been a strong point in his stubborn defense, the main objective of the marine attack of—"Was it only yesterday?"[1]

The German assault began to the right of the ridge on which Slim lay, where the clatter and clash of a pitched battle issued forth. Officers hurried toward that part of the battalion position, the better to observe the results of what was evidently a flanking attack. The first assault had been aimed at a hollow

---

1. "Just two days back he had consolidated here" refers to the night of 3–4 June, and two days later, the attack on the sixth, to which this story relates. The query "Was it only yesterday?" suggests Mackin was writing about 7 June, the day he arrived on the scene.

off to the right and out of sight among the trees; its outcome might easily determine whether or not their own hill was to be held.

Someone near at hand cried "Here they come!" and Slim's attention snapped back to his immediate front. Out there beyond mid-field, figures took shape—a long double line of fighting men formed a wave of advancing infantry. Behind, at the far edge, another took shape, and, even as he watched, a third wave debouched from the distant wood line to join the advance. Three massed lines of bayonets reflected the first rays of the red sun peeping over the horizon.

Somehow the excitement that Slim had imagined would mark a battle scene was lacking. His own line was quiet—too quiet; he could feel a mounting strain, a tension. The entire scene reminded him more of a maneuver, a sham battle, rather than an actual fight. Word passed down the line: "Hold your fire!" The distant waves came nearer. Out in front, khaki-clad figures emerged from a low thicket and fell back with unhurried steps, the men glancing over their shoulders. "The outpost is in!" someone shouted.

A rapping burst of fire came from a Hotchkiss gun close by.[1] A gap opened in the first gray-clad wave. Rifles began to crack and, as the gap closed and the attackers came on, the volume of fire increased to a pulsing roar.

Slim lay spellbound. His emotions were a mixture of fear, horror, and appreciation of a spectacle undreamed of in all his brief experience. The merging roar of rifle and machine-gun

---

1. The Hotchkiss heavy machine gun, Model 1914, was a derivative of a model designed in the nineteenth century by an American entrepreneur, Benjamin B. Hotchkiss. The French were way behind the Germans in the development of machine guns and didn't adopt a standard machine gun for their armies until 1914. Bought from the French government by the U.S. government, the Hotchkiss was not a satisfactory weapon, overall.

fire gave rise to a feeling of elation, a thrill, a mounting hysteria, which drew him higher and higher from behind his protective pile of earth to see better the panorama of courage and death depicted on that awful field before him.

Unheeded, shells burst nearby, their splinters keening 'round like angry hornets. Bits of bark spun off the trees and twigs and leaves came drifting down, but these were sensed more than noticed. His rapt vision was riveted on that scene in front.

Experimentally, he raised his rifle to cover one of those forms. They were so like the silhouette targets on the rifle range at, say, six hundred yards. When glimpsed through the small aperture of a peep sight they were nearly identical in outline, the chest-high figures of men, their heads and shoulders rising above the flood of waving grain through which they came. The difference was that these targets bobbed and swung along with the rise and fall of the terrain and were, or so it seemed, in never-ending numbers.

In fancy, Slim saw the entire German army coming toward him, the very persistence of their coming the embodiment of the horde whose name struck terror in the hearts of the Allied peoples.

Was it Shakespeare who said "All the world's a stage"? Here was a pageant of men at war. Here was a stage of magnificent setting, but with actors who did not behave like the storied men of earlier wars. Nothing was to be seen of the brave clash of bold spirits. No waving flags nor battle cries. Just a trudging mass of modern soldiery, closing in on another group of fellows who, for the most part, waited patiently for the climax of this act or phase of conflict to test in each the teaching of their trade: "Kill or be killed!"

Someone once said "One can always dream." But such a one had no conception of what war demands. In war, the dreamer has short shrift. He may from time to time observe and study, but his role of spectator must give way in time of action. In turn, the dreamer must forsake his musing to take his place on his bit of stage.

Somehow the three enemy waves had merged into one, and yet the whole was no stronger than the first wave had been earlier. Gaps opened in the surging rank and closed again, but not so rapidly as before. The line thinned, and thinned again; the air was wild with the sound of gunfire.

A fear that was almost panic gripped Slim's throat. The range was shorter, too short. With its lessening, his panic fought for mastery over reason. He felt the urge to flee, to get away. This was impossible, unreal. That thin line must go back. Damn it, he thought, why won't it go back?

A cold bleak anger rose in him. Discipline reasserted itself. It would go back! "Kill or be killed!" He reached for the tool of his trade. It came up, fitting in snug comfort like the arm of a pal. Its smooth stock caressed him from shoulder to cheekbone. Habit? Training! Target—the half-drawn breath—a finger pressure—recoil.

Target? No. It was a man, a chest-high silhouette in dirty gray, under a dome of helmet. The German staggered and seemed to sag suddenly, wearily, so close that one could see the shock of dumb surprise on his face. A hand flung out instinctively to ease the fall; then the figure settled, limp, at rest on the breast of Earth, pillowed in broken grain, strangely at peace like Purcell.

What had been a wave of charging Boche became a broken outline, groups, individuals. Some still fell, some fled, others dropped their arms to plead in fearsome stricken voices.

The sound of firing fell away, though here and there more hardened killers shot the enemy as they ran away.

Victors rose. There were readjustments, shouts, commands. Stretchers passed, carried by willing prisoners. "Dig in! You—and you. Get ammunition, quickly now!"

"They will be back again."

"Back?"

"Sure! They want this hill. Lucky we broke up that flank attack early."

An elated comrade, drunk with excitement, dropped down beside Slim. A cigaret changed hands.

"Light? Well, we sure stopped 'em 'at time, didn't we son?"

"Gee, I was scared at first. Did you see—?"

Slow puffs, a nod, an empty word or two. The elated one moved on.

The warm sun of a June morning poured over the now quiet wood. Its heat soothed and rested. Slim turned a bit to let his glance sweep the field. His look focused on a sodden bundle of gray among the others. His wandering eye was caught by the gleam of a single empty cartridge among the drying clods of his little breastwork. Its brazen shine peered back, unblinking, accusing.

Slim turned away and lay face down, his head pillowed in the crook of his arm. He feigned sleep. One can always dream.

Demonstrations

"Here they come—lots of them!" someone shouted.

Officers hurried to points of best advantage—standing openly among the clearings—to focus glasses, measure range.

Riflemen clambered up from little firing pits among the trees.

The Germans came over a shoulder of grassy hill, a thousand or more yards away, walking slowly into a sunlit valley through all the glory of a June morning. Sunbeams danced in vivid flecks of light off their bayonet points.

A breathless major[1] panted up the slope behind our line, surveying preparations, shouting orders here and there.

A Hotchkiss crew trotted up and chose a clearing, slamming the tripod into the forest loam to brace it well.[2]

Men stood about, nervously adjusting rifle slings, rising and falling along the ridge in quest of prone positions, sighting weapons, looking for an open place between the screen of brush below. Some braced against the trees to shoot from standing positions, easing their pieces back to set the peep sights to a figured range.

Somewhere on the flank, a Hotchkiss chattered sharply several times and suddenly fell silent.

---

1. This was Maj. Julius S. Turrill, Distinguished Service Cross, Navy Cross, the battalion commander.
2. It isn't possible to identify the company because the 8th, 23d, and 15th machine gun companies supported the 67th Company on that day, 7 June 1918. A gun or two from the 73d, 77th, and 81st companies were also in support of the position on Hill 142 that day.

A shot was tried by over-eager lads.

"Damn you, hold your fire!" the major shouted.

The waves of men came on, closing in across a field of knee-deep grass, trampling flaming beds of poppies underfoot.

They did not come directly to us but moved across the field diagonally instead, leaving us high above their left flank. Almost at battle-sight range, we realized the press would come no nearer to us, aimed as they were at outfits farther west.

Men craned their necks to watch the officers, impatient for the word to open fire. Even our replacements felt the urge of it.

Killing at long range is such an impersonal thing; a sporty testing of the nerves, like practice on the training range. Here was fair game. The men felt cheated.

A ragged, crashing shooting rippled down the line, somewhat like a volley, fell away in volume, then steadied into a pitched roar. We watched death strike the loose-knit ranks of walking men. Their leaders tried to charge, but slowed, wavered, and melted suddenly. Some men dropped to seek cover in the grass and set about the business of making a firing line from which to strike back; others rested quietly where they fell.

The wounded? Ah, those wounded, always optimists. Such as could walk stood up in a hail of fire to make a try for distant cover, turning their backs with seeming unconcern.

There were not so many dead, so far as we could see. Surprising that, what with all the roar of sound.

It was too far to charge with any chance of success against such firepower. Somehow we had known that, too, when first they came across the hill.

Numbers do not matter much to men who aim each shot. It seems queer where bullets go at such a time. Do very many *try* to miss? Some fellows tell you things in confidence, but you seldom hear them mention that.

Broken, the attackers suddenly started rearward. Running figures shouldered comrades from the grass. Some stumbled, staggered on, or lay quiet.

The scattered waves became a mob of retreating infantry. Some had charmed lives and wove about the place from man to man, not rattled; splendidly being soldiers.

Killers took their toll. There's always some.

We watched the last of them, the wounded, lurch and fall.

Did we forget the artillery? No. It was there, too. It came, the first rounds falling just after the rifle fire began, and broke in spotty bursts quite violently, with screams and flashes. There wasn't much of it, though. We didn't have so very many guns at Belleau Wood.[1]

Shell burst tore up the meadow, ripping off the grass to leave a black loam scar below a smear of smoke, or burrowed deep in mucky stuff to spout a flaming geyser, throwing up blobs of muddy earth. The enemy was gone at last, or so it seemed—except for some scattered figures in the grass.

A knowing voice said two Boche had taken shelter in a shell hole and tried to point out the place. It was quite far away. The fellows argued.

"See those two dead together?"

"Well, at three o'clock from there—in that big shell hole—"

"See, there—a helmet showed."

"Yeah, sure I got it. The damn bastards!"

A sniper fired—ours. He had a rifle with a telescopic sight. He missed and slipped away to find a better spot. You could hear odd shots from time to time along the ridge.

There was discussion, excited talk.

Old-timers gazed across the field with bleak, still eyes. They gruffly answered questions.

Replacements chattered nervously.

---

1. The 2d Division records indicate that the 12th Field Artillery Regiment was in support of the 1st Battalion on that same date. German artillery fire was much more intense and caused many casualties in the battalion.

"Hell, that was just a demonstration," said the skipper.[1] "They acted like it from the start. I wonder what their plan was anyhow?"

I heard the major tell a tall first Louis,[2] the adjutant, I guess, "The Boche don't give a damn about conserving manpower, do they?"

He spoke regretfully, in seeming disapproval soldier-wise, of a system that he didn't understand.

Our guns were French. Their observer talked into his field telephone, flicking his eyes from a checkerboard of map to gaze across the fertile little valley.

A ranging shot came over, fell too wide. Another went too far beyond the hidden men. Shortly, they were bracketed by searching shell bursts.

We watched this little drama unfold. One fellow clenched his nails into his palms. He looked as though in prayer as arcing shells swept down.

The two Boche finally broke cover, running, fleeing desperately toward the looming hill. We watched them separate, tiring as they struggled up the first low rise of slope.

---

1. The term *skipper* used by marines to denote the captain of their company is a salty term probably not as much in use today. In this case the reference is probably to Capt. Francis S. Kieren, two Silver Star citations, who commanded the company from 1–21 June. In a letter written not many years ago, a former member of the company indicated that Kieren's nickname was "Dugout." The tone of the letter suggests that it wasn't a friendly expression.

2. World War I jargon for a first lieutenant, rather than "first Looie," which was more common in the Second World War. The officer was 1st Lt. Keller E. Rockey, who earned the Navy Cross for his actions on 6 June 1918. He later became a general officer and led the 5th Marine Division and III Amphibious Corps in World War II. He also commanded the 1st Marine Division in China.

Snipers threw long, carefully aimed shots. The leading man went down hard, twisting in a head-long dive. His comrade jumped for cover into a nearby hole. The snipers kept up the fire contentedly, a welcome chore to kill the boredom on a sunny day.

With borrowed glasses you could sometimes see the flick of dust from sun-baked earth.

He was a canny lad, that Boche. He kept under cover, he planned to see another sunrise.

Incident

Quick glimpses at the little unimportant things, the trivia of battle, helped make us into soldiers of a sort. New to the front, more than half-scared through all those days, we pretended a show of toughness and competence, and tried desperately to survive.

Ours was not a real hardness. We were too young to be truly hard so soon. We did age fast, and functioned more or less well, depending on the individual and the leadership of the moment. We became brittle, which differs from hardness by many degrees. We were not tempered, as good lasting material is tempered, by slow fire and learned hands. We were brittle with a brittleness that was to mark all the days of our remaining lives. We were too damned young and under fire too soon.

Throughout the thirty-odd days required to clear the Germans from Belleau Wood, we replacements were fathered about through the mazes of underbrush and bits of fields by those old-timers who had survived the first two days of wild assault. Some of these were grizzled, graying men of many enlistments.

A surprising number were fellows but little older than ourselves, who had been in the outfit long enough to be real marines. Instinctively, we looked to them, for even though they may not have always known what to do next, they at least seldom betrayed that fact to us. Their cocky bearing, their sneering self-confidence and almost utter disregard for danger, coupled with a demand for absolute discipline, allowed us to follow them anywhere under any circumstances.

On an afternoon when a platoon out of the 17th Company jumped off with abrupt suddenness to take an enemy outpost, our small group was assigned to cover their left flank. We were not a squad, just a detail led by a stony-faced old-timer. We were five rifles, and while scarcely enough to cover a two-squad job, we were all that could be spared. Besides, if we got overrun in a counterattack, there were but the few of us—not too many to lose if things went wrong.

We left the firing line on our bellies, snaking away into the trampled wheat to gain the partial shelter of a shallow drainage ditch that led out and away from our front. From time to time, the sergeant would motion us to get down while he surveyed the terrain ahead and to our right, where things were getting hot. Finally, satisfied with our position, he scattered us along the ditch and ordered us to be quiet and not show ourselves. Peering through the shrubbery, we were sometimes able to glimpse a running German or two, filtering back from the outpost. They were good at taking cover, offering poor targets at quite long range.

Resistance stiffened. More and more Maxims came into play.[1] The action to our right became a bedlam of sound and fury. The flank we guarded was not threatened, so we maintained our cover.

Bullets came from most everywhere. A well-placed machine gun needs a field of fire of at least a thousand yards. Scattered shots and an occasional burst came our way— mostly wasted; stuff overshooting the targets. We kept low and quiet. There was a chance we had not been seen. In less

---

1. The Maxim gun was a derivative of a model developed by an American, Hiram S. Maxim. The German version, the Spandau Model 08, was a superior weapon and was used extensively by the German army all during the war.

than a half hour, firing fell away in volume; it was evident the 17th had taken the place and the survivors were busy digging in for the counterattack that was sure to develop. We knew they held it when a barrage of drumfire began falling on the position. Heinie wanted that outpost and meant to get it back.

When watching and not under direct fire, a fellow is inclined to inch upward for a better view of things. It is always a show, no matter how terrifying. We may have been spotted. In any case, Heinie was feeling really peevish about the whole thing and generously expended ammunition. A long burst of Maxim fire swept along our ditch, swung away, then swung back again, dropping leaves and twigs onto our sprawling bodies. After that we were quiet for a while. We could see that the sergeant had not ducked; he was keeping a good watch. But then, those fellows never seemed to scare. Not like us green kids.

A fellow can stay quiet just so long; then he has to move if only to relieve the tension. There were no more bursts directed at us, so we regained a bit of confidence, taking turns at snatching quick glances toward where the firing was diminishing.

The afternoon stretched into long shadows. Westward, behind us, the sun became a glowing ball of fire. It would be hours before full dark, but still, the day was running out. We began to fret some because we were really in no-man's-land, far—too damn far—from our battalion line. Not a good place to be with Heinie feeling as he did.

Baldy,[1] the most assured of us (none were at all brave), finally ventured a question: "Hey, Sarge?" He got no answer—not even the grunt we expected. The sergeant[2] was

1. Private Hiram R. Baldwin from Cleveland, Ohio.
2. This was probably Sgt. Louis Peterson of Chicago, Illinois, who died of wounds (DOW) on 8 June.

41

full-length out of the ditch, snuggled down in a patch of shrubs and weeds; his chin rested on his folded arms, and he was peering under the brim of his helmet. His field glasses lay idle in front of him while he studied the lay of the land toward the 17th Company.

"Hey, Sarge?" Baldy shook one foot to get his attention. There was no response. We knew better. We should not have left him there, but the evening star was glowing against the east and we were suddenly a bunch of lost, scared kids—a long way from home.

Burial Detail

By the time the question of who was to hold Hill 142 had been hashed over a few times and seemingly settled in our favor, the Germans slacked off for a number of days while their spearhead swung eastward toward Château-Thierry.

Details, working at night, gathered the battalions' dead into piles at the forest edge, opposite Lucy-le-Bocage. Some of the 67th Company's survivors of 6 and 7 June had guided members of the "damned replacements" with the harvest, having vivid memories of the road the company had taken to get their bayonets into Belleau Wood.

There were seventy-six dead leathernecks at a corner of the wood, across that first wide field outside of Lucy, and the replacements had plenty to do. Most of them had been dead for some time, the majority having died in the wheat. The stretcher bearers wore French gas masks while performing their grisly work.

During the night, the 2nd Division engineers, temporarily relieved from firing line duty, had dug a long shallow trench for the burials. Someone had to work in the trench to receive the dead, so Lieutenant Long[1] asked for a volunteer. "Tugboat" Wilson,[2] an old-time gyrene with a corporal's

---

1. There was no officer by that name on the company muster roll during that period. It is possible that Mackin confused this officer with 1st Lt. Henry D. F. Long, who joined the unit in September.
2. Corporal Earl P. Wilson, Silver Star citation.

chevrons, took the job but found the work heavy. He was patient with our squeamishness (we had been at the front only a week), and he asked repeatedly that some boot give him a hand laying out the corpses. We kept hurrying away for new burdens.

It so happened that on one of his trips, Slim passed his final exam in wretchedness. While picking up a man who had been hit dead center above the eyes, he had noted that the fellow's chinstrap was still tightly in place. When he swung the guy to the stretcher by his shoulders, the tin hat flopped off and the dead man's brains slopped messily over Slim's shoes. The gas mask was suddenly a handicap. By the time he reached the trench, burial work held no more terror for Slim. Surprisingly, it was easier and more pleasant there, being entirely in the shade.

An old-timer passing by on business of his own stopped to watch. Occasionally, as a body rolled down, Slim saw the observer's hand flick upward in salute.

After a time, as the work progressed, a body was handed down dressed in forest greens with a top-cutter's chevrons above hashmarks denoting seven enlistments. A whistle dangled loosely from a cord about the sergeant's neck, and the flap of his holster flopped about untidily.

The old-timer, still watching, made a sharp salute. Turning to a boot he said, "Get a blanket, soldier. Wrap him up proper. That's 'Pop' Hunter."

Van Calder's Voice

The evenings were long and darkness late in coming, and those among the HQ men who didn't have a chore to do would sit around the battered pits and talk things over. The fighting had swept over the area some days before and left the waste of battle all about. To us, the firing line was something far away—a quarter mile or so. We knew a temporary, brooding sort of ease.

After objectives had been attained, the major had hung his musette bag over a stub of tree and called it headquarters for what was left of the battalion. This shattered corner of a stinking wood was home.

One night as darkness fell, replacements joined us, and we drew a baker's dozen full of questionings. We thought we had the answers, and we tried to tell them things—not all quite true.

New men are always fair game, no matter what their rank, and no morbid tale you might tell them could be too far wrong in such a place as ours. For a time the talk was general and we had sport in giving information. We pitied them and tried to help them, too. Behind the banter of our cold descriptions, we knew their need and their nervousness; we also knew that we couldn't really offer any comfort. Each man had to live and learn his own hard way.

Someone laughed—too loud—to cover a quaking fear. A flat voice said, "Son, you won't laugh that way long—you'll make a pretty corpse."

We could feel the shock the new men suffered and we chuckled at them. It wasn't nice, but neither was our war; whenever a Hotchkiss rattled off to our front, we all fell silent

45

and took time out to think. It was always a recruit who broke this silence, and we somewhat resented them for it. They brought disturbing things to mar the musings of a quiet front-line night.

In breaking such a moment, someone said, "By God, I wish I could smoke." And the same voice said flatly, "You will, kid, in hell, in a day or two." At that the general conversation died down.

As is usual in such a gathering, the majority fell to listening and only two or three kept up the talk. It was a black night there under the shadow of the trees, and men became just voices in the dark.

The voice of the newly arrived sergeant began to ring a little bell of memory. Somewhere in another time and place, I'd heard him before. Kidding was over, since he was asking questions for the boots, and he got respectful answers—not because of chevrons they didn't rate so much to men up here, but because the soldier in him spoke to us. We told him what we could from our great store of knowledge gained in just a few days of life at the front.

Where had I heard that voice before, so set apart and individual and full of man-made stuff? Then it came to me: It had been that past December at Parris Island—where we boots were trained—when a squad of us, in a navy gig used for ferry work, went to the mainland for supplies. The voice fitted a red-headed stocky sort of guy who ran the boat on the brackish channels of Royal Sound.

The supplies? Two bundles of brooms, and only that, and eight young men to handle forty pounds or less. We were surprised, and asked him why.

He'd laughed that same good laugh, it was a sort of happy chuckle, and said he thought we needed a vacation—and, "What the hell, I wanted company anyway. Where you boys from?" We had shipped out from many different places and gathered there, and spoke the names of hometowns, full of pride.

The memory made a bond of sorts in the black of the woods, lighted at times by the faint glow of star shells. I took a chance and questioned him.

"Red, how was old Beloit the last time you heard from home?"

It was like seeing a fellow touch a live wire there in the dark. I was almost sorry to have startled him like that. My memory had been right, he was Red Van Galder.[1] Of all the men I knew who spoke of homes and distant towns, his pride was for the center of his universe, Beloit. When he spoke of his Wisconsin home, he made us feel it, too.

---

1. Sergeant Edwin S. Van Galder of the 49th Company. He earned two Silver Star citations and a croix de guerre.

They Will Come

The German patrol may have gone astray in the fog and bumped into our line by accident. It is more probable that they sought a prisoner or two to get information. We had one lone man out front in a listening post, and our first warning of trouble was his startled cry of "Boche! Boche!" They were, no doubt, as surprised as he. They killed him even as he yelled.

Our line blazed with rifle and machine-gun fire, and some of the patrol stayed with him. It took a long time for the officers and noncoms to quiet things because our entire sector was aroused and nervous. We did not like raiders.

Our dead man, he had been bayoneted, was brought in just as the east was showing a tinge of gray. Three Germans were left where they had fallen. It was well known in those days that our enemy always made every possible effort to recover his dead. The bodies had been left as bait. All that day they lay in the sun, a short distance outside our wire, in full view of their comrades. We got ready for company.

A couple of men who were known for having too much imagination were shifted. Their places were taken by cooler heads who would not go off half-cocked when a mouse made tumult in the grass, nor panic when noon shadows danced across the standing grain.

We knew a time of murky dark before the moon came up, dimmed by a flying scud of cloud. For the most part, we had to depend on our ears.

Have you ever tried listening through the noises of a summer night? A night when insects shrill and night winds sigh about? When distant guns make rumbling threat? The occasional *tac-tac-tac* of Maxims from way off somewhere, blotting out almost every sound except the maddening thunder of a nearby cricket? When an eerie, sad-faced moon peeks out to see, along with you, if two and one make four, or five, or none at all? If not, then you have never known *real* listening.

We strained our eyes against the shifting shadows. When we shortened our breath to harken to any stir of movement from the field, the cadence of our hearts pounded at our ears. We lay close-hugged to the earth, breathing the reek of mother soil and the mystery of night. We knew fear, and with it, a sometimes heady thrill of adventure, a lawless urge to kill. The primal man asserted his ancient call, causing the hair along the neck to stir and tingle in fear of sensed but unknown things.

Time passed. Shadows dimmed and the curling mist of dawn wove in and out before our eyes as the ground breeze woke the grass. Who knew it first? I do not know. Somewhere there were awed ejaculations—whispered, superstitious, almost fearful. "Hell, fellows," someone said, "they are gone!" We never really learned the truth of it.

It is probable that some German lad, trailing a rope from where his detail hid, crept stealthily to where the bodies lay. We can but imagine his patience and caution, hitching his gruesome burden to the line. We can but picture the quiet, steady pulling at a length of rope as the dead were drawn across a field of trampled wheat to where they could be shouldered and carried off.

Summer Afternoon

We took Belleau Wood over a period of weeks, a bit at a time. Our method of attack was a departure from orthodox warfare as practiced by European folks. We didn't confine our time of attack to the hour of early dawn, but were liable to go forward without warning at any hour of day or night. These attacks were an aggravation to the enemy in that they were always unexpected and not planned to be extensive, instead being gauged only on the ability of the men concerned to take for themselves a bit more, ever a bit more, of enemy-held territory. The quiet of a summer afternoon might be, and often was, shattered by the head-long rush of a company, a platoon, or a squad or two. The enemy found this most disconcerting.

On a quiet afternoon in mid June, the 17th Company of the 5th Regiment launched one of these attacks and took by surprise an enemy force that had held a corner of woodland for days in apparent security. Most of the affair was out of our sight in the trees at the right and slightly to the front. We could trace its progress by the intensity of fire at the initial rush and by the suddenly silenced yammerings of Maxims in the isolated strongpoints.

We who were best located to act as witnesses to the affair occupied an outpost trench where sloping meadowland came up like an arm of the sea to penetrate the woodland. We were about fifteen in number, and were very much on our toes and watchful of the result. It was interesting to watch a battle of that sort, seeing the other fellows do the fighting. I believe we were enjoying a measure of selfish security without thinking of what might be expected of us should the situation turn against our men.

As the attack reached its climax, enemy stragglers began showing through the trees on our right front as they infiltrated to the rear, away from our attack. But our rapt attention on the show before us was rudely interrupted by authority in the person of Gunnery Sergeant Eilers,[1] who said flatly, "Fix your bayonets!"

The order was a complete surprise, startling and appalling in its potentiality. When we questioned with our eyes his meaning in giving that order at such a time, he said, "When the main body of the Boche are driven out of that neck of woods, we'll go down with bayonets and try to capture some!"

---

1. Gunnery Sergeant Henry H. Eilers, KIA at Blanc-Mont on 6 October.

Outpost

The outpost had a feeling all its own. It was a spooky, threatening sort of place, full of smells. It smelled of powder and of smoke and of raw, fresh soil; it had the putrid tang one finds around a slaughterhouse. It smelled of mystery and rolling farmland mist.

Most trenches offer sanctuary of a sort and let a fellow feel protected, snuggled down as it were against the breast of Mother Earth, half-hid from harm.

In all our little time in it we never felt secure. We lived instead on nerves, beneath a weight we hadn't known before in other places.

Bushy headlands reached out at us from either side across the wheat, and both were held by German infantry. Our little trench was dug below a looming hill, in front of and outside the firing line. Though there were fellows scattered thinly through the trees along our flanks, we had a sense of being pocketed between the jaws of giant pincers, of something watching us, poised to strike.

We were, in fact, a listening post of sorts and somewhat of a strong point in advance. But then a listening post, when there is time, may fall back to a battle line to fight. A strong point stays. Our job was to hold the gloomy place, which meant staying there under any circumstance.

We held it with a squad of men at night and left it empty during daylight. By day it would have been a harvest ground for snipers, working from the headlands out in front.

We had a captured Maxim on the parapet for company. Its use was questionable in such a range-choked place, but it gave us confidence of sorts.

While keeping watch, the wiser men among us laid their rifles back along the parados, out from under foot, and fingered hand grenades instead.

In all of nature, is there any spot so dark as that black band where meadow merges into woods against a hill? When night holds threat of stalking, creeping death? Where half-seen shapes of trees at forest edge, in seeming movement, never move away, and peering eyes grow tired, and conjure things?

It's good to feel a comrade's shoulder then, to know that men like him don't run away. It's then you get the feel of soldiering.

One night, the skipper came down quietly among the trees and spent a time looking things over, whispering among us, man to man. He sensed the feel about the place, I guess. He must have known our quiet, stifled fear, because he sent an old-time sergeant down—to father us and calm us with his voice. Old campaigner that the sergeant was, he gave us confidence to face the dark. A soldier does a thing like that for amateurs.

Leaving the trench at dawn was ticklish business, always hardest on the fellows who came last. Sometimes the night mist thinned a bit before the push of morning breeze and let the flooding light of day come rapidly. It left a fellow feeling naked as he climbed the slope to reach the shelter of the firing line. Your shoulder muscles bunched in tight-pulled knots, held taut against the blow of an expected bullet, leaving you breathing gustily and deep with inner tremblings.

It's good, at such a time, to slip away among the trees behind the line; to sprawl in restful comfort on old leaves; to watch the little summer clouds; to smoke a cigaret and dream.

Quarrel Before Torcy

Soon after the "damned replacements" joined the survivors of the 1st Battalion on Hill 142 in Belleau Wood, the 67th Company was shifted to the left of the American sector. The line consisted of bits of trench and one- and two-man firing pits. These were spaced sometimes as much as fifty yards apart. It made a lonely job of soldiering, though it kept us from bunching up. Let's see now, what was the explanation? Oh, yeah, "so that a single shell burst would not fall on more than one or two men at a time." I might add here, too, that another good explanation is that we didn't have so very many men.

When we reached the hill on June 7, sixty of us boots had been assigned to the 67th Company. We had found twenty-six leathernecks left of the full-strength outfit that had first gone through the wheat behind Pop Hunter on the sixth.

So eighty-six of us had held the hill from June 7 on. We had had losses since, too. Several men were gone.

Remember that verse of the "Duckboard Trail"?

> . . . trail we know so well . . .
> One branch leads to Blighty
> and the other one leads to Hell.

We didn't have so very many men.

Hiram Raymond Baldwin of Cleveland, known as "Baldy," occupied one of the two-man pits with a boot called "Slim." About all those two had in common was an ability to use the tools of the trade.

Baldy had advantages of a sort. There had been a year or two at OSU [Ohio State University] and a good chance at football fame, but he had given that up through a strict sense of duty. For him, like Decatur, it was his country, "right or wrong."

Slim wasn't handicapped with too much of either family or education. For him, guns had muttered behind a far horizon and men he knew had gone. He had come along to see what the noise was all about. He had found the noise—and was seeing things. No one knew what it was all about.

Both men knew they were not going home again. It's a hard lesson, but once learned it makes soldiering easier.

It's probable that Baldy suffered most—good soldier that he was. It's revolting business for an educated man. He must divest himself of nonessentials and tear down to basic things. They were pitiful sometimes, these men who took clean sportsmanship and decency to France. It's such a poor way of preparation.

While the other battalions went on mopping up that part of the woods still left in German hands, grimly working forward a step at a time, a day at a time, and deaths and days all intermixed, the 1st Battalion rested easy, holding to its bit of battle line.

Then one day, Intelligence brought word that troops were massing behind the hills protecting Torcy, back of the German line. To us that meant a counterattack in force.

Well, let the old Boche come. Some few of us had watched him come before and learned that he was human and killable and much to be respected either way; a good soldier anywhere you met him. But the myth of his being unbeatable had blown away with the fumes of smokeless powder on the hill.

Because we knew he had been moving men into his lines in preparation for a call on us, the order was passed to the gun crews to engage in harassing fire. Now, this consists of firing by machine guns and automatics along the battle line—a few short bursts and silence, then taken up from strong point to strong point all across the width of an outfit's entire sector. And so, as darkness settled down, the Hotchkiss crews and Chauchat gunners took pride in keeping up the ragged rhythm of harassing.

It is a disconcerting thing for those on the receiving end, especially at night. One hears the soft *zeep-zeep* of bullets whispering by. It makes the skin tingle and nerves tighten down to the straining point. It is an insidious thing, this harassing fire, its target anything and everything; an intermittent, sprinkling shower of bits of death that comes and goes and strikes most anywhere. The Boche resented this, whatever his plans, counterattack or no. Such goings on interrupt the even tenor of a front-line night, and men at such harmless tasks as stretcher bearers, food details, etc., suffered with the infantry coming to the lines.

Soldiers hate this sort of stuff. They can face the issue of a fight where the objective may be won or lost and there is a clash of will and spirit, but the endless ripping of fire like this dries out men's souls. Subjected to enough of it, one develops an inward fury and retaliates with what he has at hand.

Retaliation came in a crushing, blinding, drumfire storm. From old experience, they knew a way to stop our show. They poured in shell fire and Maxim and bullets, too. After a bit, our line became most unhealthy and uncomfortable; quieter, too.

In the firing pit, Slim tried to sleep in a hollowed-out space beneath the parapet while Baldwin kept the watch, for watches were necessary. Raiding parties sometimes came in under cover of such a barrage as this to overwhelm an isolated spot and mayhap kill a man or two, or take some back for information.

So Baldy kept the watch, ducking low at nearby hits of heavy stuff and shrapnel, to spring erect and peer while yet he might, through fog and smoke and night into the trampled wheat to give alarm should one be needed. He kept good watch and took much risk and didn't crawl to shelter. He was that kind. No one ever had to do his job for him.

Slim, beneath the parapet, could neither rest nor sleep, and crept out against his comrade's legs to stand erect, to crouch and dodge in turn. This irritated Baldy, so they conversed, and at such a time conversation has its limitations. It consisted of high-shrieked questioning, answers shouted into a companion's ear between close bursts.

Baldy yelled, "Get down, get down, you goddamn fool! I'm watching out for us. It's my turn up. Get out of here and leave me room for dodging!"

But Slim boy didn't like it and tried to keep watch, too. He would not listen, but ducked about and stayed up, getting in the way.

There was a lull in the fire for a bit and Baldwin said, "Why don't you crawl down there and rest and let me take my turn on watch. Don't you trust that I can do as good a job as you?"

Here was pride and stubbornness and a determination to hold his place and ask no odds of anyone in a fight. So, at long last, at Baldwin's insistence, Slim boy told the truth and made it plain.

"Baldy, I haven't the nerve to stay down there and take it, for when I get it I want it while I'm standing on my feet," he said. "To tell the truth, I have had a horror that a heavy might land just forward of that parapet and cave it in—bury me alive—and I can't take that. So let me stay up here. Let me keep watch with you."

This was real understanding. A fellow spoke his piece and the other fellow knew. And in the darkness of a front-line trench, in the reek of smoke and HE gas, Baldwin and Slim clasped hands. "Kid," Baldy said, "I guess I know just what you mean."

And here was friendship, formed and forming. Not a friendship of the soft and slushy kind in which the best of us sometimes engage in time of trouble, but a friendship based on the realization of the little human fears we, man for man, try so hard to conceal.

And here was friendship, going down the roads and miles of France in mutual understanding, to a spot on a rain-soaked hill of an autumn morning months ahead.

Firing Squad

The sun beat down on the woods and wheat fields, on the few remaining battered roofs of Torcy. The weary battalion snatched at rest in preparation for the tension of the night.

Our line consisted of hastily dug firing pits and short bits of trench manned by small groups of marine infantry. Machine guns and Chauchat automatic rifles were spaced at strategic points. Some of the men slept, sprawled on the bottoms of their almost individual trenches. At intervals, lone men stood or slouched against the dirt walls of their stations, glances alert for any movement along the distant German line.

Darkness would bring bustling activity: ration and water details making hurried trips, listening posts occupied, ammunition brought forward. The quiet would be broken by the yammering of machine guns and the crash of shells. We finally had a firm foothold on Belleau, with much of it behind us after days of bitter fighting. Both sides took time to rest and engage in watchful waiting. Only the continual rumble of the guns over toward the Marne reminded us that this was but a lull in the battle.

In a clump of bushes at an outflung point of the line, two men occupied a short section of trench, its front screened by withering branches stuck upright in the freshly turned earth. The younger lay in a hollow at his companion's feet, wooing sleep, unable to rest easy.

Within a few short weeks, he had come almost directly from the transport and had been flung into the defense of Hill 142. In the dense thickets of Belleau, he had left his first dead; with them were some of his friends from training camp. Now his dozings were continually broken by the vividness of recurring scenes of horror. He wished for someone with whom he might talk.

Yesterday had been different. Yesterday he had had Baldy for company, but Baldwin had been shifted to an automatic rifle squad to replace a carrier wounded in last night's raid. In Baldy's place had come this sullen unpleasant fellow who answered in grunts or not at all, and was not friendly. Maybe, like so many of the old-timers, he still resented the replacements, looking down on them as poor recruits, not to be depended on in a pinch.

The man on watch was restless. From time to time he moved to and fro the few steps their little place afforded. There came a time when he leaned forward against the parapet, causing little rivulets of dirt to flow down, spattering sun-hardened particles onto the boy's face.

The lad craned to see and finally spoke. "What ya' doin', big boy?"

Glancing down quickly, the man replied, "Straightening this damned camouflage. Can't see through it. Thought you were asleep, kid. Better get some rest. . . ."

"That's a poor stunt. What if some sniper—?"

"Aw, hell, Mister Pershing, shut up, will you?"

The boy subsided. It seemed that most every time he spoke to the old-timers he was met with searing sarcasm. They lived in a world apart, it seemed, and couldn't see the younger men as soldiers; treated them like kids; spoke as the noncoms did back at Parris Island.

But the fool should know better, he mused. In broad daylight, too. Snipers out there with telescopic sights, who can pick a fellow out from under his tin hat and never hit the hat.

Why draw fire? Even he had learned that much. These old-timers were not so wise at that. Well, anyway, if the sorehead wanted to get hurt, let him!

The older man moved away to the end of their shelter and stood quiet. Lying on his side, the boy could see that his toes were to the front.

Keeps careful watch, anyhow, the boy thought. Well, guess I'd better try for a little shut-eye.

He drowsed off, lulled into a fitful slumber by the distant roar of the guns. The rumbling cadence became a summer shower, pounding on the shingle roof back home.

A leak? Drops? He wakened and came all the way from the dreams of home to the damp, earthy bottom of a trench on the western front. His eyes squinted tight as he wooed the raindrops from a leaking roof, his consciousness striving to recapture the ecstasy of old familiar things. The drops persisted.

He came awake to find the dust falling from the parapet again. Two putteed legs barred egress from his hole. He felt a desire to quarrel viciously with the older man. The surly coot was shifting brush again. Besides, the dream had been rapture, an experience of memory. It was hard to pass it up. Didn't he know that shells sometimes . . .

There was a rustling and a movement in the brush. Two hobnailed shoes dropped lightly to the trench bottom and the grim face of Sergeant McClain came into view.[1]

The boy's companion made a step toward his bayoneted rifle at the end of the ditch, but stopped in mid-stride, relaxed, and muttered, "Hot, ain't it, Sergeant?"

The old noncom did not speak at first. His eyes swept the parapet and the wheat beyond. He shot a glance at the boy under the lip of earth and, finding him awake, said, "Get up, son. Take the watch awhile." Then, turning, said, "C'mon you" to the late watcher.

As the boy scrambled to his feet, he sensed a tension in the men. They stood rigid, as though their thoughts clashed. The

---

1. Gunnery Sergeant Dave W. McClain, croix de guerre, who was later promoted to second lieutenant and transferred to the 66th Company, also in the 1st Battalion.

noncom's face was an inscrutable mask. Only his eyes seemed to bore into whoever met his look. His right hand hung low along his side, where a Colt automatic in a long swivel holster was strapped at his thigh. His left moved in a peremptory arc as he motioned.

"Nev' mind yo' piece. Let's go," he said, indicating the woods to the rear.

The older man glanced at his rifle. Like any soldier, he seemed loath to be separated from it. Then, shrugging his shoulders, he stopped to heave himself over the parados and crawl away. The sergeant followed.

Alone, the boy took a position facing the field, standing carefully aside from a gap in the withered branches. There had been altogether too much movement there in the past hour. Just my luck to stop a bullet, he thought. His mind followed his late companion and Sergeant McClain.

Probably making up a raiding party for tonight, he thought, remembering some of the talk of a projected party mentioned at morning stand-to. Maybe they're going to promote him. Promotions came fast in those days. Already Dailey[1] was an acting platoon sergeant, and after only two weeks at the front at that.

Somewhere back of the German lines a field piece barked. He followed the scream of the shell and mentally placed its target as back of the battalion headquarters somewhere. Heinie must have spotted movement of some sort back there. Usually, he seemed to detect every move by day, and fired plenty at night just on principle. Sure wasn't a healthy place. He studied the lay of the land in front and thought, Hope we don't have to cross that place.

He remembered crossing smaller fields when coming up

---

1. Corporal Thomas W. Dailey.

61

and could still remember the unburied dead lying amidst the grain. The patches of woods had been bad, too. Worse yet when one thought of all the dead, German as well as marine. It came to him that most of the bodies in the open were American, while in the woods they had been more evenly divided. Somehow, he wanted to get his—when it came— among the trees. The thought of shade was good when one remembered that the sun did queer things to a dead man; after a day or two he bloated and turned black.

Off to the right, a machine gun clattered. The front was waking up. Then came firing, like a volley from off there back of battalion where the shell had gone. Queer, that, he thought. But maybe an enemy plane with idle engine had swooped over an antiaircraft gun. He listened, but did not hear a motor. Strange, that firing back there. Well, a fellow never knew.

"Gee, I hope I don't have to stay here alone all night," he murmured half-aloud, comforted by the sound of his own voice. "Even 'big boy' would be better than no one."

More than one pair of eyes was needed to keep good watch at that point. After darkness came, the strain of peering into the gloom soon caused one's fancies to play odd pranks. Wooden posts that were mere posts by day took unto themselves the semblance of life, actually seeming to change position. Shadows became more dense as one stared, and it required an effort of will to keep from conjuring up lurking forms where darkness of sky merged with the murmur of waving grain.

His glance rested on the departed soldier's rifle and he felt comforted. He'll be back. He won't want to be separated from that after sundown.

After a time, he heard someone coming through the underbrush behind him. He glanced back as McClain dropped into the trench, expecting to see "big boy," too. But Sergeant McClain was alone.

"Did you get any sleep today, soldier?"

"Got a couple hours around noon, Sergeant. Tried it again while 'big boy' watched, but only dozed once or twice. The fellow was nervous, I guess. Anyway, I got to thinking and couldn't sleep very well."

"Did you notice what he was doin'?"

"No, 'cept that he fussed with that damned camouflage more than he should. It's a wonder some sniper didn't get him."

"No sniper wanted him, son. He was signaling."

"Signaling? Why, what?"

"Yep. Me and Lieutenant Blake[1] was prowling along back here and saw him moving brush. I was comin' in here to pipe that bird down, but he started some sort of wig-wag with his hands an' I took him out, and back to battalion P.C."

"Did he—?"

"—said he was a replacement. We checked the list and the adjutant looked him over. He didn't come in with you fellows. We figure he slipped in last night during that raid and borrowed a uniform off of some stiff. I'll send you another partner before stand-to."

"But, Sergeant, what did you do with him? An' what, what was that shooting?"

"Hell, kid. Get wise to yourself. That was a firing squad."

---

1. First Lieutenant Robert Blake, Distinguished Service Cross, Navy Cross, two Silver Star citations. Awarded various foreign decorations as well.

Testaments

We had come back the day before from Belleau Wood, where we lived eleven days of hell. We rested, taking out our belly wrinkles with plenty of rations, enjoying, as much as we could, the job of being in reserve.

It had been our first time in the lines. We had learned many things: the courage of the enemy coming at us over open ground; his generosity with shells in greeting any movement; the spiteful viciousness of what we called his whiz bangs.

It was pleasant and peaceful there among the trees, around the little grave-like pits that we had dug for shelter from the long-range stuff. All of us were older by a dozen years than we had been a dozen days before.

Some of the fellows slept away the drowsy June-time afternoon or lay at ease to watch the little summer clouds roll overhead between the branches.

Some sat about in little groups and swapped experiences or tried to engage our old-timers in talk, hoping they would tell about the first attacks, which we recruits had missed.

A few came in for lots of kidding because they read their pocket Testaments for hours on end. We called them hypocrites and pitied them. They were so damned sincere.

We remembered times they hadn't been, before we reached the front.

It wasn't funny.

We all had Testaments.

A loving people back in God's country had issued them to us with many blessings, and had then sent us out to fight the Germans.

They had not cared to see that we had tools of war. We borrowed most of those.

Here were men who tried to make their peace with God before they kept a rendezvous with Death.

The Germans had *Gott Mit Uns*[1] stamped on their belt buckles.

Christians are such charming people.

---

1. God is with us.

Runner Wanted

He was not like the other old-timers. When he cursed, it was in a dry, impersonal, friendly sort of way to emphasize his words. He seldom raised his voice to make his orders known. His eyes were wells of patience, understanding men.

We were glad to soldier under him. He had a way of looking deep inside of you, as though he read your very thoughts and fears, yet let you keep them hidden. He rightly cataloged most of us as boys; treating us as such, with firm and unassuming discipline. We heard the other fellows, survivors of the original company, speak of him as Dave, or Uncle Dave, when he was not around. He controlled them, too, wild fellows that they were. We replacements spoke to him as we had been trained to do, using his full title of gunnery sergeant. Among ourselves we spoke of him respectfully as Sergeant Mac. All of our platoon trusted him implicitly.

One night we came back from Belleau Wood, from Hill 142, from Torcy. Our first battle was still a recent memory. Within a space of hours we had left the firing line behind and come to this quiet grove behind our guns.

The belly-stirring tang of coffee, laced with the smell of cooking fires, had greeted us at the end of a rapid march. There had been food, more than we could eat; and water, flowing water, in a woodland stream. The men had plunged and played about like boys, reveling in the cleansing feel of it. The fellows drank and drank, and then, remembering thirst, had drunk again, lifting glowing, boyish faces from the wine of it.

Was it only eleven days since we had arrived here? Fellows spoke of comrades missing. We had been a young battalion

66

then, walking through the heat of a summer afternoon, drawing closer to the thunder of the guns. We'd been frightened too, covering our fears with bitter, quickly silenced jokes. Men seek the quiet of their thoughts when going into battle.

"Dick, you know that big, good-looking guy from Detroit; the fellow with the glee club tenor voice?"

"Oh, yeah—him. I remember. The guy who tried to teach our squad to harmonize 'End of a Perfect Day' comin' over on the *Henderson?*"

"That's the one. Well, him an' his pal, Stinson,[1] both got bumped that first night."

Voices, speaking of voices. . . .

"An' Haynes; he an' Dowdell went to the Sixth. Saw 'em both on the road this morning comin' out."

"'member the two Irishmen that always was together? McConnell and O'Donnell? Well, they got bumped too, when the 92d took that little bunch of trees. . . ."

O'Donnell, always kidding McConnell, his perfect foil. Two pals, in and out together. O'Donnell, always full of jokes about the Irish, said there were five kinds: pigpen, clay pipe or shanty, straw hat, lace curtain, and breeders.

McConnell, the serious one, once told us in confidence, "Me and O'Donnell looked over this damned war and figured we didn't like the draft."

Memory brought back the picture of an evening, far at sea, slouched on the deck of the transport, watching the day fade behind us.

---

1. Private Daniel C. Stinson of Roxbury, Massachusetts, DOW 16 June, a member of the 17th Company. None of the other names used here are in the muster rolls of the 5th Marines. Perhaps they were in the 6th Marines or even the 6th Machine Gun Battalion. There was no 92d Company in the brigade; the 95th, 96th, and 97th companies were all in the 6th Marines.

"We figured to join this outfit and get a pretty suit of blues, knock off the girls, and miss the goddamn trenches. Had it all figured—and here we are. . . ."

Yes, here they were, stinking somewhere in a stinking wood in France. Voices, and voices missing. The men were not down-hearted as they talked. They casually mentioned men we wouldn't see again. We rested that day, lying about in the shade, trying to shut our minds against the distant rumble of the front.

"Sergeant Mac wants ya." Harris,[1] the platoon runner, broke the quiet of a dreamy afternoon.

"Rest your bones, son, maybe I got a job for you," the gray-haired old-timer said, motioning to the ground. Slim accepted the invitation. "You and me have the same nickname, it seems. Made me think of you."

Conversation followed. Because gunnery sergeants don't ordinarily hold casual chats with recruits, the younger man could not make sense of it. There were questions and answers, interspersed with comments about the recent past. All the while the keen gray eyes of the older soldier weighed and probed, making estimates.

"Battalion wants a new runner. 'Itchy' Fox[2] was killed last night comin' out. They got a vacancy to fill."

Bad news, this. Not of Fox. That was just an ordinary matter, another fellow gone. "Battalion wants another runner." It came like an easily spoken sentence of death to the lad who heard it. It caught him unprepared. Snatches of conversation stirred his memory; talk of jobs too dangerous; jobs certain to mean death. Runners didn't last. Everyone knew that.

---

1. Private H. H. Harris of Keane, New Hampshire.
2. Corporal Frederick H. Fox.

Fear and protest stirred within him; tried to help him find a good excuse. A fellow didn't have to take a runner job. All a fellow had to do was say no. Except in a pinch, when there was neither time nor choice, no one served as a runner except a volunteer, for many vital things depended upon the men carrying the messages.

He could refuse and let the sergeant know he didn't have the nerve. Fact was, the older soldier wanted to know just that. If he didn't feel that he could do the job, there would be no questions asked. Suicide squad. That's how the fellows spoke of it. A runner didn't have a chance.

The noncom's eyes were wells of patience, understanding men. He read your innermost thoughts and knew your fear. He let you fight it out with yourself.

"Want the job, son?"

Could any man who had pride refuse and let that stern old soldier see the coward inside? There are some things a fellow can't admit. It makes for soldiering.

"Sure, Sergeant. I'll take it."

It was easier that way. You couldn't face the question in his eyes and tell the truth.

"You an' me have the same nickname it seems."

Thus does the finger of fate point at certain men and challenge them.

Red

Replacements always had a devil of a time when they first reached the firing line. They either learned fast, along with having lots of luck, or they didn't learn at all.

We discovered that at Belleau Wood. Any men who carried the notion that someone was responsible for guarding them from harm soon knew they were mistaken. Such officers and noncoms as were left when we arrived had other things to do. We who were to live awhile soon knew our way about, without a shepherd.

There wasn't time for a proper initiation. Men met the war and were at once a part of it, and often knew, almost too soon, what bayonet fighting meant. It was, for some, a time of much confusion.

But men are adaptable as well as expendable, and it didn't take so very long for some to find a place. Red was one of these. True, he wore a sergeant's chevrons and it may have been just that which challenged him to make his way.

The major always had an eye for men. He put Red in charge of a section of our runner group and for us it was a lucky placement. We had a risky job, at best, and needed someone who was not a martinet, yet a soldier. Red was all man, as we were soon to learn. He took the runners' work in stride and, when he sent us out, he used understanding. He did more than just roost under cover in the woods concealing our headquarters. He sometimes went along when not on duty and learned the trails as best he could and what we had to do.

It was understood all along our sector that no-man's-land was Yankee land whenever the sun went down, and each battalion strove to enforce that rule. It took time to impress that fact on the old Boche, and cost us many men, for he was as aggressive then as anyone could be. But we hadn't been battered for nearly four long years, as he had, and we were still cocky. After a while Heinie tired of the game and stayed inside his wire. Even then we were not content. We had a habit of molesting him. You see, we were all young and knew the thrill that comes with high adventure. We had a war to win and a world to make safe for democracy; but, better than that, we had a ruthless, high-handed game to play. Some men enjoyed it.

The Watcher

The hastily dug trench followed the margin of the wood, angling slightly downhill toward the ravine in front of Torcy. The Germans had overrun it before the French could string wire. Much of it lay in woodsy shade; some of it in the open sun. At night, under the late June moon, it was mostly hidden in the gloom at the forest's edge.

He was a big man, dressed in horizon blue. I had a real liking for the guy, and have never forgotten him. To me he appeared old, possibly in his mid-thirties. But then, I was still just a kid.

He had wide, square-set shoulders, somewhat like a wrestler, supporting a strong, well-shaped neck. His was a nice face, the sort one likes to see on a man. In his day he had probably charmed the women and no doubt more than a few had run their fingers through his curly crown.

His eyes were a deep blue, set wide, and the pupils were centered as you sometimes see in a picture, slightly staring. He watched you come and he watched you go. At times you found yourself glancing back to see if he was following with his look. After a day or two, you almost got used to him.

He had a friendly mouth. He always looked as though he had stopped speaking in mid-sentence just to watch you pass—as though he awaited your greeting or maybe your smile. He sat squarely braced in a revetment of trench, relaxed and fully at ease. He had only been dead a day or two.

We runners followed the bed of the trench during the day because the area was exposed to sniper fire. At night, we trotted along a path trampled in the fresh earth of the parapet.

72

Always, always you found yourself peering into the gloom of the shadowed trench, knowing he was there in the dark, waiting for you.

He wasn't a bit unfriendly, nor too frightening. Once, I had the urge to go to him, to tip him over, but I didn't have the nerve. I believe he would have understood.

Ration Detail

Moving silently, our platoon fell upon the German outpost with all the sudden ferocity of Indians. In the dark of night, the defenders had no time to organize resistance. They fell before our bayonets or fled into the sea of chest-high wheat.

The attackers had their faces blackened, their bayonets smoked so as not to reveal a betraying sheen. They knew each blur of frightened face was enemy and treated it as such. They fired no shots and took no prisoners. In a space of deadly moments, the rocky, brush-grown hump in no-man's-land was ours.

Hurriedly, we consolidated our gains and settled down to a night and day of waiting, watching for the counterattack that was sure to come.

The following evening, a detail of twenty men, replacements just come to the front, were assembled at the battalion P.C., under the command of a sergeant who was as nervous and untried as his men. Somewhere in the grapevine gossip they had learned a bit about the job they had to do. They had an honest dread of no-man's-land, especially at night, and if they had had a choice, they'd have preferred a day or two to look things over.

One heard half-conversations, muttered in the gloom, and knew from experience what their feelings were, but couldn't help. The poor devils didn't know that it was policy to break them in like that. Training and rigid discipline should see them through. Those who lived would be much better men in the practice of their trade.

They carried canned goods and bread in blanket slings, and Chauchat clips and ammunition for the Hotchkiss gun.

Bandoliers hung draped around their shoulders. Extra canteens gurgled at their belts. All this, added to their regular equipment, gave them the appearance of grotesque beasts looming in the shadows.

Van Galder moved among them in the dark. His reassuring, kindly voice gave confidence. His chuckle made the job seem casual, the usual sort of thing that soldiers did. We knew it helped.

We knew, too, that he was worried, deep inside, as we were. It is no joke to guide new men at any time. One frightened lad can cause a lot of harm.

We heard him say, "Don't worry, Sarge, I'm sending two good runners as your guides. They know the woods and trails. They've been all over no-man's-land out there. Just pay attention to them and remember, they are in command until you get back."

Organized and ready, we loitered in the partial shelter of the woods around battalion, far back of the firing line. The men grumbled among themselves. They didn't understand our long delay. Some shifted to ease their burdens to the ground; others leaned their weight against the trees to ease the strain of aching muscles.

Promptly on time, the enemy let loose his early evening load of hats, shelling roads and paths and likely places. We who were used to it could trace the pattern of his fire, knowing when he cursed the criss-crossed trails with shrapnel. We shrank in sympathy with the men around the old stone hunting lodge as we heard the enemy brush the hill behind our firing line with shells.

His gunfire fell away in volume; his machine guns rapped a final bark or two, then quieted. The men came to their feet and our little column shoved off. We hoped our enemy would keep to habit, so we could stake ourselves to two short hours in which to reach the new outpost and return.

Red said he would go with us as far as the firing line. He shepherded our detail, giving confidence to the stumbling, nervous men, raising his husky voice from time to time so they would know of his presence. Once or twice we heard his quiet laugh. That fellow had a way of handling men.

Red was worried; not so much for us, though every night when any of his men were out, he stayed up in his dugout waiting, hoping to check in all his boys before he took his rest. Many times I'd lain in my foxhole and heard him pacing.

As we approached the front, the voice of discipline, of danger, spat with venom at the ears of smiling men and slapped them into instant silence. This too, was good. We knew then for sure they'd do to take along; that discipline would have its way with them. They had smiled in the face of danger. Never again would they forget the sheer relief that men can find in a laugh.

We were at the firing line. We tramped a pace or two upon an earth-crowned bit of bridge, our footsteps sounding hollowly across a trench. We paused to let our files close up behind; heard them whisper forward from the rear, counting off. "Eighteen. Nineteen. Twenty." We knew that they were ready for the trip.

Willing hands swung wide a section of wire entanglement. Voices in the trench at our feet and in the shadows around us whispered, "Luck, old sons. . . . Come back. . . . We'll watch right here for you."

Van Galder grabbed my arm and shook me, cursing softly. "Damn you, Slim, be careful. Bring them in safe."

The moon peered at us for an instant from across the hill that hid the German line.

Our noise of passage thinned away. The men who listened heard the little sounds fade out in the gloom as we merged into the shadows of the standing grain.

No-man's-land during daylight hours was wide enough. At night, it was a blind, uncertain place. We never knew what waited in the dark.

Flatiron Island, a landmark, loomed ahead.

A sometime seafarer among the ranks had named it that. It was an island in a chest-high sea of wheat.

Let's see, I thought, the shortest way is the path that leaves the second point of trees.

Skirting the shorter western side of the hillock—peering anxiously into the blank shade, with breath half-held, all poised against surprise—we turned across the base of its lengthened triangle and paused in its final cover, closing up our ranks.

The outpost lay far over to our right, in front of a neighboring battalion. Our way of reaching it had been chosen because it allowed for a more level and quieter approach. The longest way was the quietest, and thus the best.

I was at the point, as was my place, twenty yards or so ahead, trying desperately to take it slow to give them time for careful movement, watching all around for enemy.

The sergeant had been ordered to take it easy and to remember the heavy loads carried by his men, but once outside our wire, he closed the gap repeatedly. He couldn't stand the lonely place of leadership.

Because he betrayed his nervousness by repeatedly doing what he had been plainly told not to do, his fear was transmitted to his men. It became impossible to make them keep their interval. They crowded close behind their sergeant on each other's heels, bumping into each other, determined to stay within arm's reach of the man ahead.

The fallacy of the American method of close-order drill in training was evident. Danger caused them to bunch up close instinctively when subject to command. The noise we made as a result was enough to warn even a sleepy enemy that something was amiss between the lines. Little noises sound like that, at times. We made our way across the wheat in single file, a close-packed line of frightened men.

Graded high above the wheat, the Torcy road, marked by its evenly spaced line of trees, showed dead ahead. It presented our most ticklish problem. A solid line like ours crossing its crown would cast a shadow so heavy as to catch the eye of any watcher, or present a fine target to one of those drifting machine-gun crews the Germans sent scouting around at night. They fattened on patrols that moved like ours.

I halted the men at roadside, deep in the shadows of the wide drainage ditch. It was time for all of us to rest; to gather confidence by being still; to catch our breath.

The sergeant was a threat to all our plans. He persisted in hoarse whispered questionings that reached the men. His was the only familiar voice of authority they knew and in it they read his half-stifled panic, the threat of hysteria. He would have been in better shape if he had had a heavy load to carry as they did, to take his mind off his imaginings.

Bud, the other runner, came up to join the head of our line.

"What in hell is all the noise, you birds?" he snapped.

"Look here, runner, we're going back—you fellows are lost," said the sergeant.

One could hear the stir that remark made among the men. Some started to clamber to their feet, intent on getting back to the firing line. Fully in sympathy with his alarm, those poor recruits were of a mind to follow him.

"Lost? Like hell! You damn fool, we're nearly there!"

The sergeant had his audience now and sought to cover up with bluster and authority. Anything to get away from there.

"Listen, runner, I'm a sergeant, see? Don't you 'damn fool' me. I'll—"

"Shut up, you yellow bastard," said Bud. "Your stripes don't mean a damn thing to us out here."

Secure in his following, the noncom rose and took a step toward Bud, with half-raised fist.

Bud jammed a .45 automatic into his ribs, so suddenly you could hear the breath go out of him in one hard grunt, a gasp. There was a shocked moment of surprise. The men were rigid; frozen instantly by something they could understand.

"Listen, you punk, one peep, see, an' I'll blow your guts out in chunks between your ribs."

Voices get like that, like Bud's, along the front. Something in them gives you pause. You understand.

The men relaxed. You felt at once that they had gained in confidence. They would go along and do as they were told.

"Okay, Slim, g'wan across the road. These guys are comin' over one at a time." Bud turned and faced the others. "And quiet too, you birds." A whipped snarl.

Like shadows, the detail slipped across the crown of the road. The loads they carried were like feathers in their hands. Bud and the noncom came together, quietly. The automatic had been put from sight.

The men formed up in single file; I stepped away. We walked like soldiers, not like timid sheep. The knoll, our outpost, was a silent place where nothing moved and nothing could be seen.

I had a sudden doubt; felt a biting fear.

Was this where many men had come last night? I wondered. Were watching eyes lining up Maxim guns to cut us down?

An old gunnery sergeant spoke from shadowed bushes. His gruff, old voice, half-whispering, was music to our ears.

"All right, son, just let 'em pile in here. We'll take care of 'em now."

There was a hushed-up movement as the detail dumped their supplies. The moon swam clear and brightened everything. One heard deep sighs of relief as the fellows got rid of the heavy loads.

"Hey, you guys, bring any water?"

"How about grub, Sarge? Christ, my belly thinks my damn throat's cut."

The platoon filtered down off the knoll by turns, in little groups of two and three. The men gulped a bit of water, wolfed down food, and slipped away among the rocks to keep the watch.

"All right, you birds, you think this is a rest camp? Get the hell outta here!"

"You gotta go like hell to get back now. Another damn barrage is pretty near due."

Feeling better, lighter now, we fled, drawn by the promise of shelter in our now-distant foxholes around the battalion PC. Bud led going back, moving at a half trot, just slowing down at places now and then and running out ahead, on guard for things. Ten minutes. Seven minutes. Five. The seconds raced away beneath our feet, ticked away by the schedule of the guns.

Would the firing start on time, I wondered, or earlier?

"Eighteen. Nineteen. Twenty." The whispered count told me we'd all made it safely to the firing line.

"That you, Slim? Where in the hell you been?"

Van Galder's voice.

Relief by Regulars

The left flank in Belleau Wood had been pretty well cleared of enemy. Late June found us waiting out the nibbling attacks used to clean up the remainder of the wood. By then, the battalion was much battered and in need of being relieved and taken out for rest. We had word that our relief would be a regular army outfit from the 3d Division, which would reach us in the small hours of the following night. We looked forward to getting away from that place. We had been there so long that we had lost track of the days, and of the men who had lived them. We in the outpost trench hoped to get away without any more sudden raids or pitched battles.

Sometime after midnight, we heard a scrambling on the hillside above us, and knew our relief had come. Shortly, through the gloom, figures began dropping over the parados of our little trench. Man by man we took them over, issuing to our individual relief, in hurried whispers, such little as we could tell them in the moments before we left them.

My relief was a slip of a lad. He must have been quite young. It was evident there were many things about fighting he did not know. It was a question whether he was equipped to live very long at such a location. In explaining to him the defenses of our little front, I pointed out to him the earthen pocket of grenades tucked under the parapet.

"Grenade?" he asked and held one of the lemon-shaped engines of destruction in his palm. "What is that?"[1]

---

1. This is more ironic than funny. Many troops hadn't even fired rifles before going to France. The problem became even more acute for the entire AEF as the casualty lists began to grow.

The Four Aces

Three Irish and an Ozark mountaineer; a working, laughing, serving combination. We were, for quite a time, the favored ones of all our kind. Fate, death, whatever you choose to name it, whispered often, passed us by, and in passing sometimes brushed us gently, warning us. We had, it seemed, a foil against the game. Men call it luck.

Respect and liking, common ground for common men, a mutual trust learned at risky work and during weary marches, made us conscious of the qualities each carried in his heart and soldiered by. There were a hundred little things that each one did, which served to make the other fellow understand.

Why try to put a tag on friendship, to index it, or tell why men will seek their kind of men?

We had companionship and understanding. We hiked some weary miles and knew a battlefield or two before we made mention of it; acknowledged it among ourselves.

Seeing us so much together, someone in the outfit jokingly referred to us as the four-of-a-kind—a winning poker hand most anywhere. It was a compliment, that handle, and it must have hit the fancy of the men we walked among, because it stuck. We liked the implication of it, too, and later, as our reputation grew, we had a reputation for daring, getting through, and being lucky; men who could not die. Our officers would sometimes call for us by name to guide a raiding party, get a special message out, or reach some place that others could not find.

We were no longer, then, the cowering, scared recruits of Belleau Wood and Hill 142. We had pride. We were the four aces in the runner group. Strut a bit? Sure! We were leather-necks!

We were inseparable, except when duty made it otherwise. Even then, when two or three of us were holed up snug in some safe place, there was a waiting watchfulness, unspoken worry, checking up with others, here and there, to find a missing blanketmate. We knew, however, that sometime the cards would turn the other way.

Others tried for membership. Some were people like ourselves who had a need for folks like us, and by their combat should have had a place. Sometimes we let them think that they belonged, left it to their instincts to find out we held closed membership. We had never offered it.

There were men who went away along the Duckboard Trail[1] who must have thought they had a place within our group. And, if they had lived, would have remembered being one of us.

It is a disturbing thought, to wonder now, and think of men who yearned for understanding, passing by. They had to live alone, and sometimes die, because of selfishness. But then, you cannot let many people get inside. A fellow does not know 'til afterward that little pieces of his heart will rot in graves where friends are fast asleep.

When did such a fellowship begin? It may have been below Marigny, when a still-eyed fellow name of Jack,[2] came to a wartime crossroads under fire, to guide replacements to their battle line. He had a fine contempt, just then, for folks like us. His nearest friends were killed that day, along his road.

It may have been one June afternoon, in a brief lull between attacks when we were being rested, waiting for action.

---

1. The "Duckboard Trail" was another allusion to death.
2. Jack Fackey.

Several runners, scouts, and such were lying snug against a sun-drenched bank, soaking heat into our weary bones, and talking some.

Jack, the leader then as always, took his rest sprawled in the sun. He lay with helmet-shaded eyes and spoke of things. He had something that drew men, as bits of steel will seek a magnet, finer stuff, a quality that added inches to his size. In action, he was dangerous, but just. In every sort of place, he had a smile.

Gene,[1] by then, had done a daring thing or two and won a bit of a reputation in the ranks for having guts. All of us had done our jobs with pride and felt well satisfied.

Some eager fellow, in questioning and paying tribute, too, asked, "Jack, if you were in a tight spot, an' had your choice of just one man to see it with, you'd take Gene, wouldn't you?"

For a time there was no answer. We thought for a while that he had passed the question up. Gene and all the Suicide Detail were wondering. Most of us were new men at the front, in spite of all the hell we had been through in recent weeks.

"Nope, Gene don't laugh enough, he only grins—and takes too many chances with his life. I guess if I could choose only one of you I'd take Slim, in such a spot as that."

Canny, knowing lad, that fellow Jack. He made a pal of both of us, right then.

Gene beamed complacently with that cat-that-ate-the-canary sort of look. He liked being considered reckless; wasn't a conservative in any way concerning life.

He sat, impatient, slashing at a bit of wood and smiling in his secret, quiet way. He didn't whittle, patient-pattern, as a farmer boy would do. His captured trench knife bit away the

---

1. Private Gene Clevenger.

sappy stick in jagged chunks, as though he had an urge that would not rest.

He told us often, blatantly and full of truth, that he had not joined up to die for any land, but to make some German give up life for his. Men who did not like him called him bad, a killer, and feared him, too.

He was deliberate in everything he did. Gene took time and questioned distance with his eyes before he spoke, as Western men will do.

He prefaced everything he said caressingly, with gentle oaths—"Hell, yes; hell, no"—and with music in the softness of his voice when he was pleased. In anger, he had snaggy, quiet undertones, the purring rasp that's made by rubbing callused palm on silken things that women wear.

Bud was there, I guess, among the men against the cover of the bank. It is hard to know just when he first became one of us. Sometimes I think he was the core we came to center on, instead of Jack, for all Jack's gentleness.

Bud found my diary once—a forbidden thing, against all regulations—in the litter of a billet left behind, and carried it a day or two while I was off on detached duty. Handing it to me, he quietly said, "I read it, Slim"—with no apology and just a smile for having looked in hidden places.

Bud was our anchor man, a winning, unassuming sort of Irish lad who had a job to do, a bit of war to win, and he did his duty patiently and well. In bad spots, he would dare as much as anyone.

There was a candor in his schoolboy face. An innocence that made him lovable. To hear him talking quietly of things, without excitement, it was hard to realize the places he had been or the scenes he had looked upon. Such memories did not mar his freckled face, nor dim the wildness of that open-hearted look in his deep blue eyes, beneath a shock of rusty hair that lay in curls.

Three Irish and an Ozark mountaineer: a curly headed altar boy, a bellhop out of Binghamton; Jack, the laughing one,

Ohio-born; a tall Missourian who bragged of "mountain dew," the corn whiskey made in pappy's still at home. And me? It was my privilege to walk with them.

Four aces, runners gambling with death and playing poker in a game where men are the chips.

Politicians shuffle mobs and men, and, having shuffled, deal out a generation against the guns.

The folks at home will never know the truth.

Bill

My first memory of Bill as an individual of note is at Crouttes, along the Marne River.

The 1st Battalion had come back for rest and to take out the belly wrinkles after thirteen-odd days of strenuous activity in Belleau Wood. Even here, at a range of eight kilometers, long-range shells searched for the river bridge, some falling short into the village.

We of the replacements could only claim a month or less of experience in the line, and were therefore still outside the pale of genuine approval. True, the battalion's surviving old-timers were thawing out and sometimes called one of us by name, but we had missed the attacks of 6 and 7 June and weren't allowed to claim, as yet, a place in the outfit's fighting story.

Though we had had a hand in holding Hill 142 and had helped bury the dead, some of them our own, and knew the thrill of night patrols and sudden outpost battles, we had not reached the fighting until the night of 7 June. We therefore had no memory of that direct assault at battle sight, across the open wheat, or of Maxims, bayonet bought.

Our memories of the battalion's early road were only those of spectators who read mute evidence in scattered things along the way, as we were going up.

When an old-timer waxed loquacious and deigned to tell us things, we listened, sitting, as it were, at the feet of supermen. You see, we were still "goddamn replacements."

Bill was telling things. I see him yet, expectorating sagely and condescendingly, on a rock some feet away, while his eyes were blank with seeing things of vivid memory.

He spoke of how Hamilton[1] had bayoneted four men in one swift hour, and of Eilers, who had once come through the brush in time for snapshots. He told of how Pop went down hard hit and hurt, yet rose to be shot down again, this time to stay. And of how Overton[2] went out with a Colt in either hand, charging a Maxim that was getting his boys.

Bill was telling things. He had but yesterday been kissed with the garlic breath of a "mon general" and wore upon his blouse the green-and-red-ribboned medal of the croix-de-guerre.

Although arrogant and conceited, he was a good marine, telling openly of a little history he had lived, and paying tribute to men who had died.

His own recital brought a question from a curious recruit, and in answering, I thought he lied. "No," he said, "I never in the two days knew a moment of fear."

To me, it was a lie and my lip curled in some contempt. Most of us were honest, and confessed to honest fears.

His place upon these pages is in tribute to a man who did not lie.

I concede to him a place among the only three such men I ever knew. He did not know the meaning of fear. He was made of different stuff than us. He did not suffer.

---

1. Captain George W. Hamilton, skipper of the 49th Company at the time.
2. First Lieutenant John W. Overton, Distinguished Service Cross, Navy Cross. Overton was KIA leading a platoon of the 80th Company, 6th Marines on 19 July at Soissons.

PART II

July, Soissons

Zero Hour

Pounded alert by the urgency of the march, the weary, hungry columns noted a graying in the darkness. Dawn was at hand, the front somewhere ahead.

The rain had ceased. Men who had slogged through a soaking night began to see the road beneath their feet. No longer was it necessary to extend a groping hand in utter dark to find the pack of the man in front, and so keep place.

They were almost running now. They had a rendezvous, a zero moment waiting, and they were almost late. They growled at the pace the major set. Their bodies cried for rest, for food, and for water. Tempers flared and men lashed out viciously against each other, cursing those who stumbled, who cursed in quick retort. They walked in hate and haste, with bitter thoughts about the cause of all this fuss—the enemy.

Excited Frenchmen met them at a turn in the road, gesturing frantically. The cobblestones were piled to form a breastwork there and trenches ran away among the trees at either hand. A distant, single gun barked once into the fog. A shell came screaming overhead and crashed in the trees. The column melted off the road to left and right and made a sound like cattle passing through a woodland pasture. There were no shouting voices. Platoons formed single columns, stalking off along a battered line of shallow trench, and were swallowed in the gloom. Runners gathered with the major behind the wall of cobblestones. He spoke in hushed tones. "We are in two waves, 67th and 49th will lead. A barrage will lay for five minutes on Heinie's firing line, then roll on to the first objective. Tell the captains to follow the barrage." The men stirred restlessly. The woods were quiet, deadly, threatening. It was somewhat lighter now. One could see a ways into the trees; see men crouched there. They fingered weapons nervously and waited.

"You and you, go forward with the attack," said the major. "Report back here when the companies have cleared the woods." The runners slipped away without salute. Salutes are dangerous at the front—to officers.

One instant there was silence. Then the world went mad in a smashing burst of sound. Men, caught off balance, were hurled to the earth, which shook against the guns. Minds, stupefied, refused all function for a moment and reeled. Everything within a hundred yards was gnawed in bitter, tearing bites at men and trees and wire. The stately forest melted beneath a raging storm of fire and steel. Heavy branches and trunks crushed the life from men who cowered among the roots for shelter. One heard a furious, awful screaming as the shell fire rolled away. Then mad waves of charging infantry came after it, mopping up.

Some men made the swift choice of seeing the last of war. Lone fellows gave resistance, taking a toll, and tried too late for mercy, screaming "*Kamerad!*" Some cowered in foxholes, peacefully; arising only when the victors called them up. It's safer done that way. The fellow with the bayonet gets time to think. He's not too apt to kill a kneeling man.

Men are most dangerous in the heat of their first action, back of the barrage. The let-down from the wait for zero hour, the relief of motion, and the thrill and feel of danger rob them for a time of reason, making them raving beasts. Gentle, decent fellows lose their heads and do heartless things.

Boche machine guns, range choked in the mass of wire and fallen trees, fought desperately to stem the tide, then fell silent after being rushed by steely men who took no prisoners.

Fellows who wanted to see the Fatherland again should not have stood up and pleaded so near the heated guns.

The forest was cleared. Attack troops rested while support waves passed, pursuing the enemy across open fields. The drive turned east to pass below Soissons, aiming across the base of the German salient.

"Kamerad!"

Support waves poured out of the woods, hurrying through the underbrush along the edge of the field. They passed over the line of resting men and deployed at decent intervals, taking up the drive.

A runner compared watches with his captain and turned to return the way the attack had come. He carried word to battalion that the first objective had been taken in the scheduled time.

"Next objective is the Soissons road beyond Lange Farm," the major said. "The companies may pass it before you overtake them. Find them. Check the time with any officer and return by a direct route. We will be following."

A breath of morning wind tried to thin the smell of smoke. Exploded powder left its rancid, sneezy odor everywhere. Trees died, shedding cut twigs and branches overhead. These drifted, whirling sails of leaf slowing their fall as though each fragment sought a quiet place to land amid the wreckage on the forest floor.

The great torn limbs and trunks of beeches bled, as beech trees do when cut while in leaf. Fresh-killed, they sprawled in tortured heaps or lay half-buried in the mold.

The sharp, clean, wicked wire hung broken, twisted, listless; waiting for rust to eat it into earth again.

Part of the waste was little huddled shapes that had been men.

Somewhere ahead in the tangle, a plaintive voice cried out weakly. "*Kamerad!*"

Wounded? Probably. Stretcher bearers care for their own men first. Many poor devils lay alone, untended, watching death approach or waiting for hours on end for help to come.

Might it be a trap? Odd things happen on a battlefield. Wounded fanatics have been known to exact a price for dying. Never beaten, many Germans didn't know enough to quit until they died—or took long chances, risking any gamble in attempting to rejoin their kind. There are such men in every uniform.

Fighting men respect the enemy. They never trust them. Staunch foe, the Boche. Only a fool doubts his courage. Men who know him marvel at his willingness to fight, at any odds. Trusting Heinie is another matter. Men who trust too much do not come back.

Cautiously, quietly, the runner worked his way among the fallen stuff. He had to pass the place from which the cry came. He could not take a chance on going by without investigating.

Circling the source of the sound, he quietly closed in, guided by a muffled voice that cried for help from time to time. He came upon the man at last, among some scattered rifle pits behind a rotting forest giant.

Something flopped a bit above a lip of excavation. A wounded man. Helpless, harmless, pitiful, he cried out once or twice, trying to attract a passerby.

After a period of silence, he sensed a nearby presence and turned in quick alarm to spy the runner standing over him. He babbled something eagerly, pointing to a shattered leg, and tried to lift himself above the edge of the grave-like excavation.

Having satisfied himself there was no threat, the runner turned away. He had a job to do. For a time, he heard the plaintive voice behind him crying "*Kamerad!*" It followed him a long, long way.

Bill—Again

A file of prisoners came along a narrow road. Two, lightly wounded, walked ahead. Four others carried a blanket by the corners and lugged a man between them. He must have been alive, else they would have laid him down. He made no movement.

Three others walked unhurt—a bearded man, middle-aged, and two young lads. Somehow, these personified the men we fought, the only kind we ever seemed to meet in any numbers. Most of their prime young fighting men were dead after four long years of war.

Two walked together. One had his shoulder in the other's armpit supporting him at every step, clutching with cramping fingers at his belt, half-carrying him. The helper's eyes were desperate, weary, frightened. One saw him sweat to give his strength, to aid a friend. His mate was badly hit, and walked with stiff, forced strides, pushed from step to step along the path. His eyes were unfocused, blankly staring over the heads of those who led the way. He walked in hopelessness, as though already dead.

There followed another fellow, battered by years and heavy labor and by war. He was an older man, hurt somewhere painfully. Bandages across his chest and shoulder showed fresh, red, constant stain. He swayed and staggered drunkenly and gibbered little sounds that may have been prayers.

Bill, who hadn't known fear at Belleau Wood, was herding them along the road. His pistol swung in his fist as though his charges needed guarding. He swung it easily, as if he liked the feel and weight and power it gave him.

His charges halted, glad of the chance to rest. The leaders

squatted in the middle of the trail. Those who lugged the blanket stepped aside to lay their burden in a patch of shade and kept on standing, looking, questioning, speaking low among themselves.

"Slim, if you're trying to get to the companies, give it up. You can't get through that damn barrage—nobody can."

Bill was talking. Again one had a chance to watch, to study things.

The oldster and the lads sat down beside the path and rested patiently. The helper eased his comrade down, flat-stretched upon the ground, and started fixing bandages.

"The companies are being shot to hell out in that open wheat—"

"—heard Hamilton was wounded—"

"—Elda's got a bullet in the guts—"

Bill talked, the story running from him in a vivid rush as he tried to express himself.

The older, wounded fellow settled down on a low-cut stump and braced his legs to keep from falling. His body twisted ceaselessly above the hips, from side to side. His gibberings were little whispered words. His fingers opened, clenched, and opened—suffering.

Bill was telling things. Not all of it in words. Four days or more of beard made him look wild with all the dirt and sweat. His eyes were rimmed and red and dangerous, making him look like a maddened, vicious pig. He showed the effects of heavy cannon fire and nerve shock. He showed the strain of thirst and hunger; of weariness and—was it stifled fear? He waved his pistol to punctuate and gesture, raving to his audience of one.

Time to go. There was a job to do. Bill's audience moved off a step or two, still listening.

Bill shouted curses at the resting men.

The first ones came afoot, stood waiting. The blanket bearers took their burden after trading corners—stepped out upon

96

the little road and walked a dozen paces, slow, trying to catch step and ease the sway. The three took little steps, the old one walking back to lift the helper's mate and lend a hand.

The man sitting on the stump refused to move, or tried, then shook his head in helplessness.

The former listener looked back to see him talk against a storm of curses. The gun was swinging wildly in command. It stopped swinging; sharply still, it flashed just once.

A file of prisoners passed along a narrow road.

Execution of a Runner

It came to us as a story, passed from man to man. We never knew the truth of it. For a time there were men in one of the battalions who swore that it was so. In time these passed, as fighting fellows do, to hospitals or detached duties, or slept beneath the crosses of the rest camps.

It dealt with two men of our uniform; one of them was sometimes named by men who claimed to know.

He was, they said, an officer. One of the older military school, whose kind has largely gone, and rightly so. He rated common soldiers far below common dogs, and treated them as such. There is no valid place for them today, with soldiers such as ours. The fostered spirit of America will not submit to anything but honest leadership in soldiering. At least not for long.

The other fellow was an honest lad, too young in years for war. He joined us in the thickets of Belleau Wood and learned a little war before the 26th Division took over.

In his innocence, he thought that men were equal, fair; that frankness had a place. He played the game that way; looked other fellows in the face and said his words with courtesy and courage.

Somehow, we don't know why, he became a runner. He was, in part, the type of man for that. He had a failing though, which didn't have a place as we knew duty. He dared to think and speak his thoughts. It wasn't in our scheme of things in those days, however.

The Soissons drive of mid-July swept the edge of the Villers-Cotterêts woods and raced to meet the French, coming westward through the German salient. Foch hoped to bag a German army in the trap. We didn't close its jaws.

The enemy fell back before the drive, yielding ground in orderly fashion before our rush. Their rear-guard elements sold strong points at a price and fought for time, allowing troops to form a battle line along the rolling hills by Tigny.

They halted us at the end of a bitter, sunny day and struck back viciously. Their guns laid box barrages around our advance posts here and there, and willing German infantry came back in waves of fighting men.

The youngster came up with a message for one of our embattled outfits and found it fenced in by a storm of shell fire. It was a bad barrage for any man to attempt to penetrate. He didn't like the look of it. He was not in the mood for sacrifice.

Courage failed him because he took the time to think. He knew he couldn't reach the men and, being logical, he didn't try. There were shelters around for lesser men to hide in. Dark was coming in an hour or two. Skulking places were offered everywhere. Time and distance favored him, offering the chance to plan a glib explanation. He was, for the moment, his own master, needing only to ease his conscience in the face of certain death.

He rested along the edge of open ground, watching the bursts of flame and smoke around a rain-washed gully. Men of his battalion crouched out there. His message hadn't been delivered and that worried him. After a time he slipped away to the rear, returning with his message and his guilt.

For a moment, the officer didn't seem to understand.

"Sir, I couldn't get through the barrage, it's too heavy."

The professional soldier glowered in anger, analyzing, seeming ready to burst in hot denunciation. He damned the runner silently, with eyes full of hot contempt, listening. He didn't see an honest, eager, guilty lad who spoke in full confession. He didn't hear the boy make explanation, plaintively, about the shells that barred the way with death.

The boy, frightened now, was talking against a form of hostile flesh that measured judgment; talking against cold, beastly eyes that wouldn't understand.

The officer's pistol came out with the smooth sweep of hand and arm that bespoke a lifetime of practice; easily, like a uncoiling snake, to center for an instant on a lad too young for war.

Little crosses stand above the dead. They do not tell of how men died; they hide the bitter human stories of the war. They seldom stand alone, but flock in little groups where men have passed, as though for company.

All of the dead soldiers on the Soissons battlefield share common epitaphs: "Killed in action."

They seldom stand alone. Men see to that.

Stomach Wound

The French had dug it first, utilizing the drainage swale along the road to meet the German drive of early spring. There were traces of them left: battered helmets trampled in the dirt; a rusty, needle-shaped bayonet; a punctured, flattened, kidney-shaped canteen.

The sea of wheat had looked quite different then, green and lush, promising a harvest to the early rains. Men had fertilized it with flesh and blood, defending France.

Gray-clad German gun crews had used it since for a shelter, cacheing food supplies and personal possessions in the bends and turns; spreading their blankets below the protecting walls against the burning sun of mid-July.

We came upon it in the blazing summer heat of harvest time. The wheat was a bleached-out tan; matured, unharvested, and beaten underfoot by fighting men.

The dead of three nations lay about in grotesque blots. One could trace the marks of caterpillar treads across the grain where Renault tanks had passed. Now guns, horses, and crews had gone in orderly retreat toward the horizon as the Allied drive made way.

The trench had been, for a time, a strong point of the rear-guard action, held by desperate machine gunners who sold out bitterly. Its depth, its copse of shattered trees, offered something of security and haven to weary and wounded men, who found in it shelter and a breathing space for rest. Its occupants were an assorted lot; the human froth and foam cast up by the receding battle.

The few who were not wounded spoke in quiet undertones, between long silences. They were restless, stirring about and pausing to stare away to the northeast, to where the noise of battle rose and fell. They felt a guilty sense of duty; an awareness of belonging out there, where the fighting was. Yet they were loath to leave the cover of the trench, to take their hunger, weariness, and thirst into the glare of sun.

A big Senegalese, a giant of a man, died slowly, without complaint, his great hands gripping round his upper thigh against the groin. His eyes were patient, docile, making no appeal. Rich, heavy blood crept stealthily across his big black fingers.

Under a sheltering overhang, a fine young German sat against the wall of dirt. He was neatly bandaged and not, apparently, too badly hurt. He traded glances with the men who passed. Sometimes there was a hint of fear in his eyes.

At the bend, where a shell had blasted out a wider place, part of an American squad had taken up station. One was slightly wounded in the arm. Another lay on the trench floor, on a blanket, its corners wrinkled from service as a makeshift stretcher.

They gave a grudging sort of place to the straggler who became their spectator, but they offered neither fellowship nor welcome. They were hard men, but they showed an honest grief, a clumsy, tender solicitude for their comrade on the blanket.

Soldiers school themselves to hide emotions such as grief and fear and pain. They make a bitter joke of things to cover feelings; contradicting this, if one may watch, with a tenderness and gentleness beyond all expectation.

When soldiers show an honest, worried grief for anyone to see, its source is in their hearts. They have no ready word for what they feel.

In response to a question from the spectator, one of the men answered curtly, "Stomach wound; a sniper got him."

He rearranged the dirty, folded blouse beneath his comrade's head, for no reason other than to be doing something for the stricken man. Others spoke to him from time to time, uttering the same dull, useless questions:

"How's it going, Jim?"

"Are ya' feelin' better?"

"Want your head up higher, fella?"

Putting hope into their voices. Pretending a reassuring smile, while their eyes betrayed their worry and fear.

It was easy to see Jim had a place with them. One like him had a place in every group. Somewhere on the road he had given each of them some word of comfort or a glimpse of understanding that they had treasured.

There is always a Jim in every lot of men.

The soldier who had described Jim's wound suffered too, giving his mate all of his attention; from time to time, growling the others away from too close importunings, knowing in his heart the uselessness.

Anyone could see that Jim belonged to him. The picture they made showed buddies and blanket mates, a bond which only men may know. These two were close.

The wounded man rested easily, with little movement. A gray band of paleness rimmed his thin-lipped mouth and one could note the vise-like set of jaw and watch the nostrils quiver as he fought against the shock and pain for breath.

His eyes were clear and fully open, surveying every little place and movement, showing nothing of alarm or fear. Sometimes there was a trace of wonderment, of questioning, a man's eyes asking, "Why?"

Suddenly, the stricken man retched violently and quickly turned his head aside to spew a flood of crimson. He gasped and choked and tried to smile. The hemorrhage weakened him. He seemed to sink more flatly against the breast of Mother Earth. "Water," he murmured weakly.

Canteens came out. The fellows moved with eagerness to give a helping hand. A willing arm encircled struggling shoulders, a canteen poised, shakily guided by the hand of the weakened man.

"Don't give him that!"

It was the spectator. Something in his voice arrested motion for a space of seconds while they gave him time to speak.

"Don't give him water. They taught us that at the training camps. Water and a stomach wound might kill him instantly!"

He spoke with such conviction that men believed him. They hadn't even thought of it. In fact, maybe they'd never heard. In any event it sounded reasonable. He must be right.

The issue was settled by the wounded man himself. In spite of his burning thirst, he felt assured. He accepted the advice, relaxing his palsied grip to settle backward on his pillow—surrendering to reason.

Not all the others felt the same about it. There were disbelieving growls, doubtful looks.

Who was this buck who dared to interfere in looking after Jim?

Damned straggler. Dog-robbing runner, by the look of him with that brassard around his arm.

One could sense their thoughts in their hostile glances. They wanted peace and quiet. They wanted time to rest away from hell; to care for Jim, for he was theirs.

For a while, there was quiet. The scorching sun of afternoon narrowed the edge of shadow below the parapet, pushing away the shade of broken trees.

There was no cover from the heat, yet everyone clung to the shelter of the trench, protected some from the high-explosive stuff that sometimes broke along the road.

"*Water!*" It was a dried-out, whispered plea for comfort, not to be denied.

A comrade whipped out his canteen, the motion sloshing the precious fluid about inside the thing, which sounded empty.

"Don't give him that!" Emboldened by his early victory, the spectator reached out to take command. Even as he reached, there was sudden motion. The canteen fell unopened and, like a bird of prey, an arm swooped down then up, bringing a Colt automatic into sight.

All knew a frozen moment.

Death swung down to hover above the trench, to brush across the faces of the men; to squeeze the muscles of an arm and white-knuckled hand.

To pose expectantly—

"He drinks, Buck, see?"

The spectator backed away a step, not answering, distended eyes full-centered on the pistol's muzzle. His breath expelled gustily in deadly fear. He could not speak. His belly muscles cramped at the awful shock, then uncoiled reluctantly.

Jim drank. The delicious stuff relieved his pain. He thanked them with his eyes and tried to force a smile. He rested quietly. The moments passed—

There was a sudden, bitter retching; again, a crimson rush of blood. After a moment of protest, an age of resting peace. Men were motionless as they watched their comrade die.

Before the spell was broken, the spectator, white-faced and shaken, slipped away around a bend of trench, grateful that men had dug it there.

Two German Boys

Even under the afternoon sun that trench was a fearsome place. Walking along the nearby road would have been easier, but long-range heavy stuff slammed in from time to time and made it risky. Bad as the going was, the trench offered a place for hurried cover, so the runner followed its winding turns toward where the Allied drive was rolling eastward.

Short hours before, the enemy had paused just here, to offer rear-guard action. The tide of battle rolled across him, driving his battered units to the line of the Vierzy hills. Now there was bitter, brooding peace, lulled by the guns of the receding battle.

The man walked in fear. Death had brushed his shoulder recently, in passing. His tight, drawn nerves still tingled at the memory of it. He hurried away from something deadly left behind.

Movement caught him napping. In a short swift arc, his pistol swung up to cover a gray-clad form. He paused; there was no danger.

The automatic sought its holster noiselessly, as though in shame. The runner sat down along the parados, to study things.

A stricken thing was watching. Sensing no harm, it clawed the face of the trench, despairingly. It soon found its feet, came lurching nearer, talking with its terror-tortured eyes. It wanted only company.

Hit low, the German boy had no chance of living. His guttural words could not be understood and, realizing this, he quieted, gripping the stranger's hand.

Rested a bit, he sought to rise, pointing along the trench. Lending his shoulder, the runner helped, half-carrying him.

The objective was a body, one of several. Lowering himself, the dying boy gave full attention to the dead.

Here was the explanation in a still, small figure. Brothers! The same fair hair; light blue, kindly eyes; mold of features. Were they twins?

The German dropped a hand in slow caress across the brow of one with whom he had been in the cradle. He had won to his last objective.

"They are Marines"

The force of our drive spent itself in the wheat fields and on the little rolling hills that flanked the Vierzy ravine. Resistance stiffened along the German line and it was time for those in command to survey the situation and find out what the sunset hours had left for us to do. We had advanced about five miles.

There was, of course, confusion. The troops were all mixed up and some had gone too far in pushing the retreat. According to the maps—and there were too few of them—our drive had broken down in places and left important objectives in German hands. One of these was Vierzy.

The headquarters group had trailed behind the fighting and been at times entirely out of contact with the rapidly moving line, although runners had come and gone all day. The field of action was very wide and some had been unable to find the battalion in a country overrun with men from three divisions.

Late afternoon found us filing past two ruined farms, where we could see there had been some bitter fighting. We approached by way of a valley the converging lines of hills between which Vierzy lay. Our troops were somewhere out along the flanks, held up by machine guns in the town.

We who were with the officers at the head of our column were greeted with some hurried shots as we rounded a shoulder of hill beside the road and we took cover in the ditches. The major broke out his map and held a hurried consultation with his second in command.[1] A man was sent away to borrow

---

1. Captain Keller E. Rockey.

108

a platoon or two from where they might by spared by our embattled companies. Waiting, we crept up to see the lay of the land. We drew attention from a sniper and then were content to wait for reinforcements.

It didn't look like a good place to venture into and it wasn't our kind of a job—so we thought then.

Behind us there was a raucous horn blast and the noise of men giving way. A staff-car, army manned, slid to a screaming halt.

Before it stopped, an irate lieutenant colonel jumped out and made himself known as his darting, wrathful eye sought and found our battalion commander.

"Major, just where in hell are you or where in hell do you think you are?"

"Here, Colonel, see"—The major pointed to his map in explanation. "We've been held up and—"

"Held up, hell, you were supposed to have that town by four o'clock, and here it is six-thirty and the sun is going down! Go get that—"

"But sir, I've sent for help from the companies. I've got to have some men."

"Men? Men? Jesus! You want men? What's the matter with all of these around you in the ditches here—are they Boy Scouts?"

"But, Colonel, these are runners, clerks, and orderlies and such as that. They're only armed with pistols and I've only forty, more or less. They can't—"

At that the colonel made a silken purr, loud enough for all to hear; you could feel his satisfaction. One could easily picture someplace where we gyrenes had stolen glory and a fair share of the news from this old soldier's own good army outfit.

That grimace was, I guess, a smile. He glowed, and was so human that he took the time to catch the eyes of men who listened, softly saying, "They *are* marines, aren't they, Major?"

"But, sir, you see—"

"See, hell! I don't give a damn if you only got twenty of

them, they are marines, my dear major, and I'm ordering you to take that goddamn town!"

"Aye, aye, sir."

We knew then that our old man would take us and our pistols into town.

Butt Stroke

We were not a combat outfit as combat outfits go. We came from all the battalion units; from other outfits, too. We were scouts, liaison-telephone men; there were some navy hospital corpsmen and an orderly or two. The runners went along of course, as runners do. Some of the men in the companies who watched us from the flanks said later that "even the damn dog robbers can charge, when they hafta."

Somehow we made a running skirmish line and hit across the backyards of the town. We were scared enough to make it look like we meant business. Some men picked up rifles as they ran. We reached houses, most of us, and then all hell broke loose.

From a steeple deeper in the town, machine guns opened up. Another started firing from the red-tiled wall of a factory, and shortly German shells were dropping in among the buildings where we hunted. They did damage to their own as well as ours.

Someone yelled. "The factory. Look—!" A handful of men rushed it and some got in. The Maxim stopped abruptly. There was bitter, hidden action in the place. A shell in lowering arc burrowed under the feet of a man running across a garden, crashed, and spun him backward through the air in cartwheel fashion. Two men grabbed onto him to get him into shelter. He was twitching horribly, his eyes rolling up and showing white.

There were prisoners, lots of them, although plenty hadn't known enough to quit and many fellows hadn't cared for those who did. We gathered them in the factory courtyard from all

111

over the town. They were cocky, eager-looking lads who really didn't know that they were whipped. They looked us over, sizing our numbers, weighing things. You could see it in their eyes.

This was the day the tide turned. 'Til then, the Boche had been winning all that summer, except in local actions here and there. They were very willing, looking us over.

I had a German rifle and stood guard with two other fellows. We could feel the strain and read their thoughts. They were not like other prisoners we had known.

Then we saw the why of it. There was a German captain, working in and out among the mob, saying things. He was laughing. You could see he was a leader of men.

I've often wondered how he knew to pick on me.

He broke ranks, sauntering over and saying, "Gee, I'm glad you fellows captured me. I'm from Chicago."

I stiffened and told him to get back.

He kept on coming. "I was in Germany on business when the war broke out. They dragged me in—" He stopped short, trying to make it sound casual.

How did he know me for a softie? Me, trying all these weeks to win a place with men, and getting places, too. I didn't want to hurt him, but I had a job to do.

He broke out cigarets and offered them, talking American like anyone and stepping out toward me. We had a space between us of about seven paces. I told him once more to get back and choked a bit. We both could feel the strain. He didn't stop. He laughed, shakily, his eyes gambling everything he had. He knew somehow that I didn't know my trade. His smile was thin and white, down in the corners. With the cigarets extended in his right hand, he measured things and flicked his eyes from mine—a flash—to see just when to make the snatch. He was a man, and I thrill to think of him.

Two paces more. We both knew it. Willpower couldn't take it; he couldn't hold the pace—he stepped in fast, too soon to grab, still smiling at the point of a bayonet. I did something

112

then a good gyrene would never do, but then I didn't like their war—I stepped back a step, then gave him what he asked for.

The butt stroke caught him squarely below the jaw. I knew that part about my trade full well. He landed on his shoulders, quivering. Two of his lads came out to drag him in. I hope he didn't die. I liked the man. I often think of him and wish him well.

"I Bet They Was Surprised"

We had swept through Vierzy and the Vierzy ravine and were occupying what we later called "Buzacot Hill," just to the northeast and above the cemetery. The defense stiffened up, consolidated some, and made ready for counterattack. We were not in numbers and the old Boche were, and evidently they were feeling sore. We were to do what we could at long range, sniping, but the wheat was high and the terrain rolling, and we knew that should they come as they had at other places, we were sunk. As Heinie's attack wave formed across the wheat, we settled down to firing; there was a feeling among us that even if we held 'til he arrived, the effort would be in vain.

At about this time, when needed most, a battery of 75s manned by Frenchmen dressed in horizon blue debouched from the valley below the town and came loping toward us. Their course led to our right and away along the ravine, but a runner moving rapidly got them stopped. They made a quick survey of the situation, loosed their guns, and set to work in almost nothing flat. Their well-placed shrapnel caught the enemy in midfield, stopped him, broke him there, and sent him back. The German artillery was quick to retaliate and, directed by a Fokker plane up above, soon had the range.

Amidst the guns, four French officers chattered excitedly around a yard-square bit of map spread on the ground. A shell of goodly caliber crashed down suddenly, exploding just where men and map had been. Of men and map there was but a reeking hole, smoke-clogged and rancid. No other trace was left.

We were startled by a burst of hearty laughter, and turned to find Gene Clevenger, the Missouri mule, arms crossed over his belly, rolling in the wheat in an uncontrollable spasm of mirth. It wasn't funny, yet we had to smile. His laughter was infectious, and while we puzzled some and could not understand, we joined in, too. At long last, after the paroxysm had subsided somewhat, we asked for an explanation.

Gene tried to give it to us through his chuckles and tears.

"But, Gene," someone said, "What in hell—just what in hell was there to laugh about?"

Half convulsed, Gene pointed weakly down and gasped, "Oh, Jesus, I bet they was surprised."

Drama

Men show the effects of battle in different ways. Most take to their road in still-eyed, wary watchfulness, content to move along with events, unhurried, poised, their senses keyed to meet things as they come.

Others slog along like stupid beasts, their eyes half-glazed with weariness, their faces masks that blank away their thoughts.

Some show a nervousness, a tight-lashed strain, a hope that they can hide their fears from men. They suffer most because they choke on dread. They snap and snarl at things that soldiers do, that soldiers see.

Another kind just make a game of it and get a thrill. They have an eagle look, like birds of prey, a hungry questing for the joy of hunting things. Because there is no law except to kill, they find pleasure in the job of killing men.

Our firing line was along the edge of the wheat field, just at the brow of the hill above the Vierzy cemetery.

As soon as the 75s broke the back of the counterattack and the German infantry began to retreat toward Tigny and the Villemontoire road, the enemy machine guns began a covering fire from the flank in an effort to keep us down and protect the retreating men.

The bullets made noises like angry hornets *zeep*ing overhead or popped like champagne corks near our ears when they were close.

Occasionally, a head of wheat would spin down from its stem, as though an unseen sickle had snipped it from the stalk.

Most of us were glad to see the Germans go; we were

mighty satisfied they hadn't got to us, and were satisfied to let them go in peace.

Two reckless Yanks stood full-height in the wheat, disdainful of the bits of singing lead. They had their aim and proceeded to kill with carefully sighted shots, placing their bullets in the backs of running men.

They played a game, keeping score. You could hear them shout at each other now and then, a note of exultation in their voices.

"Got five, got five! Hey, Lem, I'm catching up—"

"Yeah? Hell, I missed that bastard. Ah—got six—"

The lieutenant was one of our nervous, tight-lashed ones; he'd seen enough that day to last for life.

"Get down! Get down, you two! Take cover there."

Neither took the time to turn his head.

"C'mon, you men, get down!"

They played their game. It was a sporting test by now, at long range.

"Got six! Hey, Lem—"

Fearfully, frightened at the urge that drove him up, the risk—hearing those *zeep*ing, stinging sounds—the lieutenant came afoot and raised his voice at them.

"Damn you, you goddamn—men, I said get down—"

The nearer man, a lanky lad from Athens, Alabama, turned slowly aside. He lowered his rifle, loosened up his sling, and looked regretfully across the field of grain to where distant figures ran toward the trees.

"—under cover, you men! I—"

"Lissen Lootenant, don't be a-cussin' me, ah don't want any man talkin' to me like youall was."

His voice was cold, deadly gentle. His eyes were still, deep pools full up with threat; he had an eagle-like look, a glance that pierced as though he sought to whip himself, to dare.

You watched the killer in him writhe and crawl.

Three men. A deadly drama. On stage.

The other man, the sniper, had his way. "Look here, Shavetail"—spoken in cool contempt—"you're at the front. You don't amount to a hell-in-all up here. Y'see, Shavetail, a man can get killed easy 'round here, even a lootenant, an' he won't smell a damn bit better'n a common soldier after a couple a days—got me?"

Home

Buzacot Hill was home to those of us who lived to hold it. We dug down deep and made ourselves secure. Some men go to great pains when digging in and take pride and joy in having things secure. Others dig a rifle pit with a pile of dirt at the firing end, and let it go at that.

The type of foxhole, pit, or trench a soldier makes is somewhat indicative of him as an individual.

Red Van Galder dug himself a nice, deep hole. He had room enough for another man, at least, and someone coming by said, "Red, you've got one *bonne* sector there!"

"Yeah, it makes me think of home," drawled Red.

"Think of home?"

"Yeah, it's so damn different."

"Step Out, Old Son"

When the German counterattack broke in midfield, one of the Boche took shelter in a hole and, as the front quieted with the passing of the afternoon, he must have begun to worry about being late for chow. He suddenly burst into full view like a startled rabbit and headed straightaway across the field toward Tigny.

Clevenger, ever watchful, swung down on him and we waited to see him fall. Instead, those near at hand heard Cleve mutter, "C'mon, old son, step out. You're slowing down." Then, with cool deliberation, as the tiring man kept stumbling on, he placed a bullet square between his running feet and made him jump. With that, the man really began to run and made a grotesque figure going away from us.

Again we heard the "Old Mule" say, "Come on, son, get them going." Again his bullet flicked between the flying feet.

The German's objective was a gouged-out bit of wall on the outskirts of the village of Tigny. The trail he followed led straight to it and we who watched knew he was running to his doom. Clevenger was a killer. He didn't let them get away. We knew in our own minds that he was playing the old game of cat and mouse and having himself a little entertainment.

As the man neared the break in the wall, we heard Cleve say, "Now, once more, old son, you better jump." There were two quick shots and stucco flew from either side of the opening in the shattered wall as the terror-stricken man dove through the gap. Gene was laughing.

120

The eager, knowing voice of some recruit wishing to sound tough said, "Hell, Gene, why didn't you kill him while you had the chance?"

"Aw, hell, he gave me some fun," said Clevenger. "Let him get away."

Acceptance

We learned to close our minds to the memory of men who fell.

We took the way of living day to day, and braced our inward fears toward some vivid time and place when we in turn would fall, and be, we knew, forgotten in the column.

We learned a kind of laughter; a bitter, joking, careless sort of stuff that free folks can never understand. It suffered and served its purpose, masking fear, blanketing out our little man-made hopes. We learned to laugh at everything in time. It carried us.

A battalion is a thousand fighting men—before a battle. They are just an average lot of fellows, coming out of many ways of life to serve, they think, a cause. Knit by discipline and service into a compact unit, their only common denominator is their youth.

"That's the Hell of It!"

During the night, the Senegalese and some elements of the foreign legion took over our line. Just at dawn, the Big Red One (1st Division) deployed in flowing waves out of the northwest, joined up with the French flank, and movement started toward Tigny.

Our battalion—what was left of it—was taken out of the assault. We were in better shape than when we had come out of Belleau Wood two weeks before. There were more of us. We'd had replacements twice.

My company slipped down off Sea Bag Hill, that knoll of trampled wheat just east of the Vierzy cemetery. We kept to the lee of the buildings as we wound through the town, for some long-range stuff was coming in. After we passed the smashed church at the junction, we felt safer. Our pace slowed as we picked our way across the fields toward distant Villers-Cotterêts, where we had jumped off two days before.

There had been some singing during the night marches, coming up. There was no singing now. We slogged along under the blazing July sun, each man busy with his own thoughts. Debris along the road held little interest. Burial details were busy, but they had not yet gotten to the Germans and the horses. Those horses sure smelled to high heaven. You watched as you marched. These were some of the men who had sung "Tipperary" and "The Long, Long Trail." Route step was automatic; the easy, strength-saving pace of veterans. The faces had changed. It would have been easy to attribute the differences to weariness, hunger, and thirst—to the caked sweat and grime. There was more in those eyes than these.

There was recent remembered horror, framed within masks of week-old beards.

When a youngster stumbled, and let out a sob, one of the hard-bit older ones threw a quip—a stab of joke—but took the kid's rifle for a spell. His joke was probably old in Caesar's time, but still of use among fighting men. The older ones knew how to stifle grief. We were a ragged, dirty, wire-torn crew. The step quickened as we neared the shade of distant trees.

The lad who had yielded up his rifle was naked to the waist, sunburned hamburger raw. Blobs of broken blisters sent rivulets down his shoulder blades. He wore his breeches snug and tight below his hips. A belt of white turned slowly pink above the trouser line, below raw-rubbed ribs. From time to time he swung his carried cartridge belt from hand to hand, sheathed bayonet bumping hollowly against the empty canteen.

You listened as you marched. Knowing kids, coming back from their first action, viewing the man's nearly bleeding back, commented wisely, "Gas. He sure got it bad."

We knew better; it was only from the sun. It didn't have that greenish-yellow look. His back would heal, but his scars would be deep, and never, never leave his eyes. He wouldn't ever be truly young again.

As we slogged west into the afternoon, the battle rolled east. Time and distance muted the guns into distant thunder. Horse teams, dragging cannons, churned clouds of dust against the growing dusk.

At Longpont we picked up our 10 percent, eager for news, looking for missing faces. They were our first "ten per"—that proportion of any combat company left behind by army order, before any scrap. I don't remember the exact language, but it dealt with a new policy, whereby no outfit would ever quite be annihilated again. We had not left behind any at Belleau Wood. It seems it wasn't good to send total news back to the States; bad for civilian morale. Then, too, it always left a few from each platoon to build upon.

"The kitchens are up, guys, just inside the woods. Plenty

of grub, guys. Christ, we been drawin' chow for a full company ever since you fellows left."

We ate like hungry hogs. There was plenty, too. We were anything but a full-strength company. One pictured the weary mule-team miles the field kitchen had come since we had hurried off. Had we only been six awful days away?

Gunnery Sergeant John Johnston met us at the edge of the trees, running an old-timer's practiced eye through our thinned-out ranks, maybe looking for a face or two. You never knew. Our mess sergeant and more—our "John-o." Where we went, he followed, determined to feed his men. Why, back at Belleau Wood, he even brought the kitchens up through Lucy-le-Bocage to the back of Hill 142 at night, fed what was left of us, and got the teams back to Marigny Château by daylight.

By early evening, we were settled along a woodland road. Stragglers joined up and working details returned to formation. Officers and noncoms buzzed about calling rolls and counting noses, detailing guards—getting on with the business of soldiering.

Some men slept as soon as they were fed, but most of us, still drunk with the fever of battle, lay about and tried to still our nerves with talk.

You watched and you listened, for these were the men of your outfit, and they had a thousand stories.

"Salisbury? How about Salisbury? I heard he—"

"Naw, he wasn't. A shell spun him ass over applecart just as we went toward the first house. Wasn't dead, just knocked plain nuts. They took him out."

"How about Hill, Glayron Hill? You know, the Carolina boy?"[1]

---

1. Private Glayron E. Hill of Mt. Carmel, Illinois, DOW 28 July 1918.

125

"Yes, bumped. Sniper got him outta the steeple."

"I saw 'Fats' Hall get it through the legs from that damned church, I was right behind him. I . . ."

They had a thousand stories.

A quiet voice took over. "Damnedest thing I ever seen. One of those kid replacements—right down there by the cemetery wall, where 66th Company took its stiffs. He was layin' on his arm, like he was asleep, and some guy had took a shirt, and made a tent over his face. Damnedest thing I ever seen."

You watched. You listened. And you remembered. That's the hell of it.

Part III

August, Pont-à-Mousson

Oil

This is in no part an ad, but it so happens that we Americans —both as men and boys, most of us—having grown up with firearms as commonplace items in our play and amusement, have in mind one particular brand of oil when we need some for our tools. This holds as true for the soldier as for the civilian.

In the excitement of the campaign of 1918 there were times when we were far away from our base supplies. Or perhaps the powers that be neglected to list some essentials. In any event, we occasionally knew shortages.

We came to a time such as I have described in the middle of the summer of 1918, when we were getting ready to take part in the drive on Saint-Mihiel. The battalions were desperately short of oil for the small arms and, being troops of character who took great pride in the condition of the tools of our trade, we worried some about the lack of lubrication of our pieces.

It was not all pride, however. First, it is a matter of common sense and good soldiering that pieces of any type shall be kept clean and well oiled for appearance's sake and for inspections. Then again, some will not fire properly unless they are oiled according to the manufacturer's directions. While a Springfield may be worn and used in the bone-dry state to the detriment of the piece, the automatic pistol may easily jam and totally cease to function if even so much as a wind-blown speck of dust lodges in its working parts.

There was thus a continual demand on the part of the troops for our old reliable 3-in-1.

After weeks of want and worry, a limited supply of the necessary lubricant was received and, because we had known shortage and were on restricted ration, the little bottles were distributed only to the Hotchkiss and Chauchat crews.

We other poor recruits, who had a feeling of great respect for our campaign pieces, were forced to curse and beg of these favored men in order to keep our weapons in repair.

At such a time, I fell back on Baldwin, found him busily engaged in hand-polishing the gleaming bits of his dismantled Chauchat gun. Daring to take advantage of his comradeship, of months of close association, I bummed a bit in asking for some oil.

Because we were men, and because we had shared much of common memory, he paid heed to my request after sending better men away and said, "Well, yes, because it's you, I guess I can allow you some, but that stuff is precious."

In joy, I unlimbered my .45 to administer to it a badly needed bath. I was generous with the precious stuff, but then, to me, that gun was precious, too. Like other good pals, it had gone places with me and it may be that it had brought me back.

I was generous and Baldwin caught me at it. The howl he raised was something to hear. At some length, he said, "And you call yourself a soldier, wasting stuff like that. If you were a gunner or anything but a damned dog-robbin' runner, you'd know that just four drops of that would clean up any piece you ever had."

Allemands

We were in the Pont-à-Mousson sector early in August, giving front-line experience to a host of untried men and getting the division into shape for trouble yet to come.

It was a quiet place, held by *Landwehr* divisions of older men and by outfits shattered in the crushing drive of March to May—from the Chemin des Dames almost to the very gates of Paris.

Beyond a raid or two, organized to "blood" young officers from the replacement troops, we had not very much to do. Just hold the line and soak up strength and enjoy the summer sun.

The runners free-lanced, going here and there and getting by, along the front, on the strength of arm brassards and stern expressions.

Just wear a worried look and move along, as though on heavy business bent, and MPs[1] will not stop you. Don't dodge them, pass them with a sneer like those worn by front-line men—but do not tarry. This was still the front, however quiet, and MPs are made to be fooled.

Some visited other outfits to check up on home-state pals last seen on a dawn-lit road at other places. Others slipped away to Belleville, to a grog shop there, though that was taking chances.

We had a patched-up, brooding sort of peace. The few shells came from way back and gave good warning as they fell

---

1. Military policemen.

almost lazily on open ground. It was a *bonne* sector, and the boys were apt to wander.

There was a sun-drenched slope of grass-grown hill behind our first battalion and, when we could, we prowled the edge of it among the trees. Along that slope we marked stark bits of weathered board, sentinel-like, scattered here and there, and went to see.

A running tide had come in waves upon that slope and foundered. A gray-green tide of fighting men, now four years gone.

Here was the high-water mark of the highest tide to reach for Nancy and the railhead there. Here again was a place where men had said, "They shall not pass."

Waves had come here, and crashed, and broke, and crept away, leaving a reddened froth to be buried.

The sentinel boards stood knee-deep in ranker growth of weedy vegetation, over filled-in craters where giant shells had blown. In stark memorial to gone and vanquished men, each board held a headstone legend, *Allemands.*[1]

----

1. French for "Germans."

A Dip an' a Dash

Lying around that quiet sector at Pont-à-Mousson, mostly in reserve, we got the first and only rest of that summer. The outfits drilled every day when not on stand-by, gradually welding the new men into the squads and platoons of the rifle companies.

We guys of the battalion headquarters group sure had a dog-robbin' time through those days. As long as a runner or two was within the voice of the major or adjutant, ready to take a call, the rest of us were free men; freer than we'd ever be again. We looked up old pals in the other battalions or visited the 6th Marines. Once, a handful of us took a chance and, taking advantage of the red brassards on our sleeves, we went so far east along the front one afternoon that we ran into a Limey outfit, like our own enjoying a quiet bit of front. That was my first and only visit to an English canteen. They didn't have nearly the choice we could find in a YMCA. All they could spare was a few biscuits.

One afternoon, the Moselle tempted us. We hadn't had a swim, a dip of any sort, in one hell of a long time. We knew better, but that water sure looked enticing.

The river came away from the German wire in long, looping curves. Though the woods along the stream had long since been shattered into desolation, the damage had been done earlier in the war, when the Germans were making their month-long bids to flank Verdun. Since that time, the scrubby willows had made a growth of sorts in shallows, bits of islands here and there. One loop of water faced a high dirt bank in no-man's-land, screened by brush, we thought, from German eyes.

133

We forgot the war. We played and frolicked in the limpid warmth of an August afternoon, splashing each other like the boys we really were. It was good fun.

Of course, it didn't last. We got careless. One or two of us ventured far outside the shelter of the bank and Heinie took exception to our fun. The shells, just three or four of them, came screaming toward us, telling us to move ourselves away from there. We took our own good time at leaving, too, for we damn well knew that German battery didn't want to do us any harm. Had they meant business, the shells wouldn't have landed so far away. German artillery didn't miss by that much.

That whole country was full of men in those days. None of them were doing any fighting, either. Both sides used that sector for a place of rest.

We drew more than shells that day. We drew a mess of cursing military police who tried to pinch the bunch of us. But, hell, we were infantrymen, and you can't chase a foot soldier through the woods with a damned motorcycle. We had been chased through better woods than those, by tougher men, in other days.

"Dinty"

Every outfit has its "Tugboat" Wilson. Every outfit has its "Dinty" Moore.

We had helped Tugboat, an old-time gyrene, bury seventy-six marines and five Germans in a trench near Lucy-le-Bocage, back in early June. That was when "Pop" Hunter was buried. The five Germans? Well, our engineers had dug a larger, longer trench than we really needed that day and we were policing up the place. Somewhere along the road, since then, Tugboat had "gone west." I never did know when or where.

We were lying along a pasture fence, somewhere east of Nancy, where we had detrained some days before, watching our share of the 6th Replacement Battalion come dust-kicking up a valley road to join us.

Me? I was from the 3d Replacement; got to the front in early June, saw most of the thirty-three days of Belleau Wood. Here it was August. Private Arthur Moore and me were dog robbing a bit, keeping away from the drill and killing time.

Dinty? He was from the 4th Replacement. They had joined us in Belleau in time to see a lot of that place, too. I had met Dinty just once, shortly before I went overseas from Parris Island. I had found him on a YM bulletin board and, because he hailed from Ransomville, I looked him up. He was even younger than me.

Funny thing about war, ain't it? Here he came into Belleau, where most of the old outfit got hit, and got assigned to my 67th Company, like me, a replacement. I was a couple weeks ahead of him at the front. Of two marine regiments, and our machine-gun battalion, Dinty caught my outfit, even my old platoon. Funny thing about war, ain't it?

Sixth Replacement? Christ, where had the outfits gone? The 1st and 2d had gone from PI before I finished boot training. I'd come over with the 3d; Dinty, here, with the 4th. The 5th? Hell, I never did know. They got to the front after the Soissons fight. I guess they all went to the 6th Marines. The 6th took a real whipping at Soissons.

Now we were on the Pont-à-Mousson front in one of the French armies, again in what they called a "defensive sector." Truth was, we were so all shot to hell after Belleau Wood and Soissons that they had to send us to a quiet front to rebuild. That was why we were waiting for the new men. We were badly under strength. Lying there on our chins, looking down the road, I chuckled.

"Yes, they are funny, ain't they?" Dinty said. "Did we ever look like them?"

"Yes, son, we looked like that. Once, not anymore. Kinda pitiful, ain't they? Clean, healthy, well dressed. Christ, I wonder if I'll ever live long enough to wear a gyrene uniform again. I get awful sick of this army khaki. Look at 'em. Gawd, but they're young. Was you ever that young, Dinty?"

"Aw, ferchrisakes, Slim, knock it off, will ya? Young? Hell yes."

"I was laughing about something a long time back, way back last May, before we got to the front. Dinty, how long since you kidded any Germans?"

"Kidded Germans, Slim? Don't be funny. Nobody kids those birds—nobody but those slacker bastards in the SOS![1] They don't know any better."

"Hell, neither did we. I kidded Germans, once. I'll tell you about it sometime."

---

1. Services of Supply.

PART IV

September, Saint-Mihiel

Drafted

We looked like army men. Our forest greens had gone at Belleau Wood because we looked too much like Germans at a distance—and suffered casualties from our own troops because of it. We wore the army uniform, and only an occasional insignia here and there on pistol holsters, caps, and such identified us as Marine Corps—until you heard us talk.

We were proud of many things, not least of all the fact that we were the outcasts of the AEF—the leathernecks. We kept our fierce self-conceit and pride.

We had been hiking nights, closing in on Saint-Mihiel and keeping to the cover of the woods by day to hide the preparations. One drowsy afternoon the word was passed that a draft of replacements was joining us. For lack of other things to do, we gathered along the road to look the new men over. About two hundred strong, the lads from home came up the road out of the valley. They had detrained at a nearby railhead, so in spite of the training camp packs they carried they were not too tired to strut. As they passed along our ranks, the kidding started. Replacements are always fair game.

"Bet that bozo over there thought he was goin' in the navy!"

"Oh, oh, the famous 'First to Fight' eh? Christ, you're late—we won the war last June!"

"What bunch are they? The Cuban volunteers?"

"Devil-dogs, eh? Leathernecks—"

A cocky, strutting kid took up the quarrel, as we had wanted. The others, slick and trim in their green uniforms, just passed us up in cold contempt, walked straighter, struck a pose of dignified soldiering.

"Another bunch of MPs—gyrenes. I heard the YMCA sent for 'em."

The cocky kid? If his service record said he was more than seventeen years, he had sure lied to the recruiting sergeant.

"You're goddamn right we're leathernecks, you sons of bitches, you! Yah! Look us over, army—you drafted bastards. . . ."

Like a Dose of Salts

Which was your favorite Liberty Bond poster? Was it that one with the tall, young lad returning helmet-laden from the front and carrying the caption, "And They Thought We Couldn't Fight"?

The veterans of War One had to make their choices of posters from among the weathered and windblown remnants that still clung to the sides of billboards and barns in 1919, after the world had been made safe for democracy. But it so happened that I met that lad in person in France.

It was on 12 September at Saint-Mihiel, just a little outside of the jump-off point at Limey-Remenauville, east of Montsec. He came back from either the 9th or 23d Infantry, the outfits that were leading things for the 2d Division that day, and he brought word that things were going well.

Tall, blue-eyed, and blond, he came striding back across the field of battle to greet us with a smile. He was still drunk with battle fever, and it must have been that his wound hadn't begun to throb yet.

True, he was somewhat out of his poster character just then. The shoulder load of souvenir helmets was missing, as was his own, along with the rest of his equipment. A shattered arm clung sling-wise through his buttoned blouse and a ruddy bandage swathed his upper arm and shoulder where the uniform had been cut away.

Some eager recruit greeted him in passing with, "Hey, Buddy, how's things goin' up there?"

His answer brought a laugh. "Aw, hell, son, goin' fine. We're goin' through 'em like a dose of salts through a tall, thin woman."

Lovely Lady Refugee

We were a flowing tide of men that day, hurrying to join a moving battle line that even then was lapping at the slopes of Montsec, deep in the Saint-Mihiel salient.

Refugees in endless streams came out of Thiaucourt and Jaulny. Women, children, and aged, withered men jammed the roads, fleeing from four years of German occupation. Along the way they met us, their Yankee liberators. Stricken, fearful, harassed folk, they fled away behind our moving waves. They seldom paused. One sometimes read a swift uplift of greeting in their eyes. Peasants? Tradesmen? Little folk like that. All but one.

She led a flock of not-so-hurried folk, with chuckled cluckings, like a proud old mother hen; with confidence, a sort of bright "I told you so." One read it in her poise. She had a faith, a place apart from those she shepherded. Her flock was of mothers, puzzled little ones, a patient, stoic *grandmère* here and there, and some ancient fellows, watery of eye, bent low beneath great loads of precious things. All knew her leadership and traveled quietly in her command.

A lovely lady. No one needed to question her estate in things like that. She was an aristocrat in every movement she made. Children clung against the folds of her quaint dress, like little chicks that look for mothering and love in time of storm. She led them at a quiet, steady pace as old campaigners do when roads are long and weary, when strength must be conserved and speed is set to accommodate the weaker ones.

Our major was a huge Apollo of a man.[1] Time had been when the fellows spoke of him as "our motion picture captain." That was before he bayoneted four men in one swift hour, way back in June. Kind spoke to kind, with eyes that knew the strength of gentle blood as heritage.

The major? All six-feet-four of him was deference to Her Ladyship. He made a picture there, doffing a battered metal helmet, easily, with natural grace, as though his topper had swept to greet a miss at Eastertime. He bowed, as a humble, cultured gentleman does to womanhood.

With quiet, easy confidence, she drew him down, one small hand grasping at his Sam Browne belt. She kissed him soundly, once. That was for all of us, or so her merry glance said. We took it so. Her people looked on smilingly, without surprise, as though they knew her foibles, loved her ways.

Did any other fellows ever see a smile among the streams of refugees in France?

Came quiet clucking, words in French we fellows didn't understand. Her people shifted to the ditch to let us pass.

Her hands, like lovely petals, brushed our sleeves in swift caress. There was a merry twinkle in her eyes. Wrinkles from a life of smiling lighted her face. She let us go, leaving us with a vision of the mothers of our race. The men walked in silence, seeing yesterdays.

---

1. The battalion was by then led by Maj. George W. Hamilton, a brave and efficient marine who had command presence and a handsome appearance. He stopped what might have been a rout of his battalion on 4 October at Blanc-Mont. He left the Marine Corps after the war, only to return in the early 1920s. His untimely death in an air accident terminated what should, and could, have been a distinguished career.

Thiaucourt

The town lay off to our right rear, two or three kilometers away.

The major said, "Son, you see that steeple over there among the trees? That's Thiaucourt. You'll find our regimental train just west of the town—it should be there by now. Tell whichever officer you can find I want a water cart up here as soon as possible."

Our drive was going well, almost too fast. The schedule of objectives, planned to cover two full days of fighting, had gone by the board some time before, as all well knew.

The 9th and 23d regiments, which led the fight for our division on that day, had long since abandoned the program of the clocked attack in an effort to keep contact with the retreating enemy. Afternoon of the first day had found them closing in on the base of the salient.

We had followed them for hours at walking pace, enjoying the show, and only lost a few men along the way. We found the backwash of the battle interesting.

The men were hard to handle. They tried to drift away in little groups in quest of souvenirs. Or they lagged behind, intent on searching for dugouts, gunpits, or any spot that caught their fancy for a time.

Older fellows scoffed at replacements because they walked in awe and half in fear.

"Hell, man, ya shoulda been up at Soissons."

"The old Boche fought us there."

"Why, kid, this ain't no battle, just a walk-away for troops like us. We'll maybe chase them bastards to Berlin."

144

"Hey, runner—you!" the major yelled. "You walk behind that damned water cart the whole way back. I want to find it full when you get here."

Thiaucourt was something to behold that afternoon. Traffic was tied up in hopeless knots. Baggage wagons, ammunition trains, everything that goes to make a drive, was jammed in snarls that growling men profaned from every side.

Authority, in Sam Browne belts, was everywhere. Bewildered shavetails shrieked against the din, and irate colonels added to the row. Old soldiers cursed them back impartially and made no choice when voicing their remarks. Rank was just a sweating, swearing joke. Here and there, some still-faced officers surveyed the scene and quietly moved portions of the mob to end the confusion. Every road, it seemed, debouched upon the village square and ended there.

Trains and columns, batteries of guns, everything that was an army on the move had poured into the place as though into a funnel and gotten jammed into a helpless mass.

Stragglers hunted busily about the place and looted every room of every house quite openly. The only complacent ones were the mules. They didn't give a damn for anything, only swished their stubbly tails at swarming flies and stood, slack-footed, patiently at rest. It looked as though the creatures smiled.

America was just a little more than seventeen months at war with Germany that day. For the first time since the declaration, an American army, by name, was in the field, and Thiaucourt was just a little village, an isolated spot in our first mighty battle.

I wonder what the history books would say if the Germans had counterattacked that afternoon. Is it any wonder that Foch delayed the business of assigning us a section of the front to call our own? Or that the British said we were a liability along the battle lines.

By late in the afternoon of 12 September, the Germans had gone back as far as they planned to go. They stopped at chosen

145

positions. We stopped, too, as we always did when Heinie stiffened up.

The German *avions* again took over the air, coolly chasing off all Allied planes in sight. It is certain that some of them spotted the mess in Thiaucourt.

Long-range German guns took up the job of adding to the confusion. Shells slammed in among the buildings with a roar. Thiaucourt, beneath the urging of the distant guns, emptied itself in a disorderly manner, like an anthill with the lid kicked off. The story goes that a week later some groups were still looking for their proper places.

Later still, the regulars were making jokes about the thing. Whenever someone raised the question as to the whereabouts of outfits or individuals or ranking officers, the answer was liable to be: "He (or they) is still wandering around the fields at Thiaucourt, looking for a battle that got lost!"

Stretcher bearers are usually very reliable fellows, although once in a while they do funny things. There were casualties in Thiaucourt, of course. A dressing station was located near the center of town. A pair of stretcher bearers carrying a wounded man were making their way toward where the sawbones were, when a salvo of heavy shells landed in the row of houses along the main street. Whole walls seemed to lift beneath the blast and literally move outward through space, only to fall in heaps of smoking dust and stone into the street. The stretcher bearers dropped their burden and ran for shelter, leaving the poor wounded fellow lying in the open, gazing upward at a narrow strip of sky between shaking walls that threatened to come down on him. Almost at once, two other men ran out to where he lay, grabbed the stretcher and hustled him through a courtyard to the partial shelter of a garden wall.

Both rescuers were loud and vehement in their remarks about the men who ran away, but the injured man felt different about the thing.

"Yeah," he said, "I watched the sons of bitches run and

146

didn't blame them much, but I kinda wished that I coulda gone along."

The runner never did find his regimental train. Fact is, those were four hungry days at Saint-Mihiel. We lived on apple butter, rabbits, garden truck—but that's another story.

Jottings at Jaulny (Part 1)

We moved into Jaulny in the last of twilight. The hills where Heinie lay, to the north and west of us, were shouldered up against the afterglow of sun.

Within the hour, the roar of battle muted down to the mutterings of distant guns. Machine guns yammered now and then against the quietness, but couldn't raise a chorus of reply to their excited barkings.

The armies rested sullenly, in weariness, and took time to lick the wounds of that mad day. They welcomed dark.

Jottings at Jaulny (Part 2)

The château had served a dual purpose. Primarily, it had been an enemy hospital, secure and safe beneath the great red "mercy" crosses painted on the roof. Conveniently, it was also a German headquarters of sorts. Old soldiers know the use of things like that.

Most of the rooms to the right of the main entrance hall held hospital beds. We fellows dumped our combat packs on these and staked a claim.

Names of men, their regimental designations, and type of wounds were listed on the cards that hung below the footboard of each bed. It was funny to see "Woody" Wilson, a laughing Yankee fighting man, take his ease on a comfortable mattress and insist that "My name is Rudolph Younkblutt, an' I got a pistol wound, see—jes' read my card. Besides, I don't *sprechen Sie Englisch*. I'm a sick woman and in no shape for soldiering."

Our room evidently had been the surgery. Another, near the back of the place, held hospital supplies.

Across the hall, the rooms and furnishings told quite another story. The kitchen was a marvel of a place with a great stone fireplace built along an inside wall, opposite a mammoth kitchen range. Utensils hung about in neat array. Great cupboards held dishes, brassware, glass, and cutlery.

Beyond was a long narrow dining-living room with a table large enough to seat a number of persons comfortably. There was a scattering of broken china on the floor; fragile stuff that broke beneath our feet like eggshells. Linen, silverware, and such as that was missing. Whether the retreating enemy had taken it with them or our own souvenir-hunting infantry had helped themselves, we never knew. We had a feeling of disappointment and resentment when we, searching, failed to find it for ourselves. Such loot was always good for food or bottled goods or entertainment—stuff like that.

Two bedrooms, furnished well with pillaged odds and ends, made up the suite. The beds were huge canopied affairs with full, thick feather mattresses. They stood so high above the floor that little built-up steps were necessary to climb into them.

Great, odd-shaped, massive mirrors had a place. One mirror leaned from the top of a spindly legged table, resting against the whitewashed wall. It trembled, ringing, when larger shells landed nearby. Another had a heart shape, like an ancient shield or coat of arms. One could see the old varnish stains along the edge of it, where the frame had been. It stood point down on a great, wide dresser top, anchored in a deep-gouged crevice hacked in lovely wood. An upper corner of the glass was broken.

There were some clothes about the rooms: field gray uniforms, a pair of boots, some clean-folded linen on a closet shelf, and a dirty shirt or two. We found some woman stuff. One soldier held it up and laughed, "Them bastards sure had one *bonne* sector here."

Jottings at Jaulny (Part 3)

When our battalion headquarters group took over the château, we found some jobs that needed cleaning up to make it livable. Shells had struck the stable. A mare with a half-foaled colt was lying in a stall, still suffering. One of the fellows put a bullet through her head. Sprawled half out the door, a big, black horse had died across the threshold. There were also several goats that needed burial.

Nearby, in the courtyard, was the body of a German officer. Two dead German lads were found in the wooden hospital ward in the east garden. All had been killed within a matter of hours, probably while the place was changing hands.

Dead horses are heavy, awkward creatures that are mean to handle. After some strenuous tugging, we succeeded in dragging the animals out of the stable and into the large garden on the south slope behind the château. With entrenching tools and other equipment we found about the place, we finally disposed of all the objectionable debris; a large shell hole served as a common grave for everything.

When the men finished their work and began walking toward the garden gate, a heavy shell struck the corner of the main building, killing two of them.

Sergeant Smith,[1] who had direct command of cleaning operations, surveyed the situation for a bit and said, "Hell, fellows, more work! We may as well bury them now, then all of us can go get a drink of water."

---

1. Gunnery Sergeant Charles J. Smith, two Silver Star citations and the croix de guerre.

Goat Milk

Only once in all our time along the front did Jack get mad. He took a lot of kidding for his pains.

We were hungry. The field kitchen, ration carts, all the divisional train, as well as the ambulances, must have been stuck in that traffic jam at Thiaucourt some days before. We hadn't had a meal since God knew when. True, we scrounged about the gardens of the town and found potatoes, turnips, cabbages, and such, but they were poor substitutes for monkey meat and goldfish, bacon, coffee, and slum—the kind of food a doughboy thrives upon.

Jack was a versatile cuss. Among other things, he knew his cows.

We had found a flock of goats about the place and for a time had fun watching them. After that we had our fun with Jack.

No one ever questioned the charm of his personality, not even the old nanny goat that he made advances to—in quest of milk. He had a way with females any time.

He made quite a picture: patient, gentle, kind, as he wooed and won and had his way with her, balancing a canteen cup in one hand, milking with the other, taking time to slap her kids away.

Finished at last, he set the brimming cup on the ledge of the stable window and then, considerately, he took time to toss some hay to his pets.

Jack was hungry, famished to the point of weakness, stirred up by his appetite and by the smell of warm, raw milk. His face was a picture of anticipation as he came through the stable door: dignified, serene, unheedful of the raw remarks the spectators made—although some of the things they said had gotten inside his skin, as anyone who knew the lad could tell.

Nonchalantly, Jack strode through the group toward the cup; self-satisfied, he reached to slake his thirst.

He gaped speechless, then turned to the rest of us with sparks in his blue eyes.

The boys had drunk the last damn drop of milk while Jack was throwing hay to the animals.

"Goddamnit, C'mon!"

Midafternoon. The rifle companies lay in fox-like holes along the Jaulny-Xammes ridge and cursed the burning heat of the sun and their burning thirst. They cursed the German flyer who swooped down along the line from time to time with raking fire. Otherwise, it was a quiet day.

Across a valley, far enough away to make men look like crawling ants, a trench line took form. The enemy was digging in along the base of what had been the salient.

The sound of single, sullen firings rolled along the summer sky and died in mutterings against the quiet of the front. A small, well-hid gun barked out at times with vicious voice, from underbrush that cloaked the valley floor.

The major, wanting a prisoner or two, planned a raid. When observation failed, we took that means of getting information about our interesting enemy.

Did you say, "Would they talk?"

Listen, bud, when a couple of our tough guys started working on a prisoner, he was damn glad to talk.

I took a sealed message up to the skipper of the 67th Company with orders to deliver it to him personally and promptly.[1]

Lieutenant Ball—say, that reminds me—I never saw Lieutenant Ball again after that day.[2] It's funny how the little

---

1. By that time Capt. Frank Whitehead, Distinguished Service Cross, Navy Cross, Silver Star citation, croix de guerre.
2. Lieutenant Clarence Ball, Silver Star citation and croix de guerre.

things a fellow does, come back. He gave us chocolate one time, at Belleau Wood. Anyway, the lieutenant said the skipper had gone down beyond the ridge on a sightseeing trip into the valley.

Now, who was that big shavetail leading the platoon? You know the one I mean, that big rah-rah football player, the one we fellows always thought was yellow? Anyway, he showed me where the skipper slipped outside our line through some bushes, and I went down to look for him.

Delivering sealed messages is like that. You don't take chances on delivery to the second in command or anyone else. Sure it was risky. It made a fellow feel damn queer crawling downhill into no-man's-land in the middle of the afternoon. Of course, you went as though you got a kick out of it—adventure stuff, you know. The fellows on the line were watching me, and that damn shavetail was, too. You had to act as though you liked it. When you're a runner, you have to act cocky about such things. Besides, the skipper was down there, wasn't he? And I had orders—

If you don't think it's a lonesome feeling, just try it sometime. Just crawl downhill on your belly with enemy in plain sight over there and see how you feel.

I had my automatic in my hand. Of course that was silly, but it helped my feelings. There's a lot of confidence to be had from the feel of one of them things. It helps like hell when you get into an open place and think of snipers. Naturally, if one spotted you, your .45 wouldn't mean a thing. Them damn snipers are good, I'll tell you.

I used every bit of cover I could find. You know, a little bunch of grass looks inviting as hell in a spot like that. It makes you understand sometimes—especially when you close one eye and peek around a couple of blades of grass.

Guess I was out a good five hundred yards from our line, down flat, when I spotted the skipper. He was sitting face first in a little Christmas tree with his back to me. I remember thinking about that tree. It made me think of my kid brother and sisters back home. It was about five feet high and perfectly shaped. We had one just like it one Christmas.

What? Yeah, that was a damn funny place for a captain to be, but we had a lot of officers like that. Our major was like that.

Sure, I know. Plenty of officers wouldn't have the guts to get out in front of their own men. We had plenty of guys along that line that could hit an eighteen-inch target nine times out of ten at six hundred yards. It was different with our skipper, though. Our whole bunch would go to hell headfirst for him. He wasn't in any danger—except from the Germans.

I guess seeing him made me hurry. I could have gone around that open place and got there, but I was feeling jumpy. I just crawled on my elbows, dragging my toes, and I went fast.

The skipper had a Springfield with him. When he swung around, that rifle just jumped right at me and looked me right in the face. You know, that's a hell of a feeling—looking into one of them things. That cold eye of his didn't look good either. After a second, he just grinned a little bit and nodded at me to come on. Guess I scared him some. His face was kinda white. He read the message and stowed it away in his pocket.

"Tell him okay when you get back," he said. Then, "Take the glasses, Slim." He dropped the strictly military stuff lots of times. "I been looking 'til my eyes ache. Watch that patch of trees. They got a damn whiz-bang in there some-where; got three men so far. I was trying for an hour to get a shot at them."

Somewhere a distant gun barked once. A high-arced ranging shot came over and exploded behind us, back where I had come from. The skipper cocked a questioning eye at it—and me.

"Suppose they spotted you?"

Another distant bark. The screaming squeal of it was closer than the last and suddenly we knew it was meant for us. We crouched down close for an awful space of time and held our breaths.

156

"Christ, that was close." We flinched as clods came plopping down on us and stung; we breathed like men again. There is no feeling quite like that, knowing another shell has passed you up.

"Yep, they did," said the skipper, answering his own question. "Goddamnit, c'mon!" We made knots going up that hill.

Sniper

On the face of it, the town was ours. We thought our comrades in the infantry had mopped it up. About the second day, we figured otherwise; too many men were dying in the square. At first we hadn't paid attention. Shells were slamming in from time to time, and when we runners noted new dead on the streets we thought the guns had got them.

I don't know how the question was raised exactly, except that someone died; someone who had a pal that cared enough to look for him, and found him with a bullet through his head.

We knew then that a sniper was about; was picking off lone men who crossed his sights. They sometimes played a waiting game like that instead of crying "*Kamerad*," as the wise ones did.

We knew, too, that the bullets came from within the town itself. The German firing line was out of rifle range beyond a hill. The bodies and the bullets told us where to search. It's not so hard to figure things like that when you know which way a victim was headed and note the angle of fire.

An old-time sergeant brought a squad down from the ridge to search the place and, because some of us runners were underfoot, he put us to work, too. There is a thrill in hunting men. It's a greater sport than hunting rabbits anytime—rabbits can't shoot back at you or call your bet.

With a little experience a fellow soon throws off most of the softening influences of civilization and becomes an animal of sorts, after which he is free to enjoy himself as best he can.

War is just a high-class type of poker. That's why some fellows learn to like the game. "Kill or be killed" just means you play for keeps. There are mental protestations sometimes, but they are easily submerged by the call of duty.

Our men were feeling cheated, too, for the drive had been a disappointment all the way. Just an overgrown sham battle at best. Under the circumstances, none of us were very hesitant. We didn't care for snipers in the least, and besides, the fellow we were seeking had, by his own acts, made his choice.

Our search centered on two short blocks of stores with living rooms above them on one side of the little village square.

The sergeant put his detail to work along one side of a block and assigned the other block to the runners, scouts, and signalmen of our detachment.

Most of us were glad to work in twos and threes because a fellow needs support on such a job. There's something in the fact of having company that lets a fellow do his stuff in spite of fear. It was different with Gene. The lone-wolf hunting strain was strong in him. He ranged alone, cat-like, moving quietly from house to house; he didn't seem to mind the ringing emptiness of vacant rooms.

Three of us were making a careful search in a three-story place when suddenly we heard two close-spaced shots nearby and hurried out to lend a hand, to see what—

Even as we ran, there came four more shots—slow, deliberate firing, the kind a fellow makes when he has lots of time.

Gene met us on the stairs and waved us back as he came down—almost indifferently, as was his way. We heard him shout, "Okay, Sarge, got him." Then Gene sat down under the arch of a doorway and cleaned his .45.

The Kid from Michigan

Harley, the kid from Michigan, lay on a bunk in one of the deep cellars under the château. He couldn't hear the big shells breaking overhead around the place, searching for the river bridge below the wall.

A single smoky candle sputtered in the neck of a bottle. Its light made shadows dance across the faces of the refugees, who crouched in corners waiting, watching with a stoic, quiet calm. Van Galder was on one knee beside the boy, with an arm wrapped pillow-wise beneath his head. From time to time he shifted a dirty wet handkerchief or dipped it in a crock to moisten it again before laying it across the boy's fevered brow. They were talking intermittently.

The kid fought to hold on to reasonable thinking. It is difficult when pain and shock have taken their toll for two full days. The boys had stopped the bleeding from the wound above his knee and now took turns keeping it bandaged. They had no means of easing the pain, which now was a dull and endless burning throb all up his leg and across his lower back. The ambulances had not been able to get through the bottleneck where the road wound between crowding hills above the lower valley. The shells broke there with steady, deadly fire.

"I'll be okay, Red. I'll be back with the battalion in a month or two—"

"Now listen to me, brat," the sergeant said. "Some of us have been talking. No matter how good your leg gets, you limp. You keep right on limping, see?"

"Aw, hell, Red, I'll be okay. They say it didn't get the bone."

"Damn you, listen to me! You're just a kid. You don't belong in this game. You oughta be in school. Now you keep limping, see? You keep limpin' 'til you get back of that old Statue of Liberty and get a discharge."

"Now, Sarge, look here—"

"Christ, kid. You been through Belleau Wood, an' Soissons, and now this. Get out of this game while you still got a chance. Let some of the damn slackers with weak hearts and flat feet come over here. Let some of the damn politicians—" The sergeant stopped and fished in a pocket. "Here's twenty francs an' my wristwatch, son. I won't be needing them. You go get a couple of drinks for me when you get out of the hospital, kid, and don't come back. Keep limpin', see?"

The boy laughed. It seemed he always laughed at everyone when he wasn't singing. He had a startling way of jarring weary men along during the hikes, picking arguments that brought up smiles.

He made a joke of everything along the road and tried to sound hard when talking about things that he had seen. Men loved him. He was the kid brother of a thousand leathernecks.

He laughed. "Hell, Sarge, you're a hell of a funny soldier talkin' like that."

"Sure, kid, I'm a hell of a soldier. I wish I had the guts you've shown. An' listen, punk, I been talkin' with the boys, see—any of us catch you back around the front, we're gonna kick your ass clear up over your shoulders, y'hear?"

161

Officer's Woman

A few of us who had business in the old wine vaults and cellars tending wounded had glimpsed her by the dim light of the candles and, soldier-like, had felt her presence, though she gave no sign of seeing us. Once I found her hovering over the bunk where Harley lay, but she moved back among the shadows with the huddled refugees.

I asked the kid about her, but he was burning up with fever from his wound and really had not known that she was there.

On the afternoon of the third day, the shelling slackened. The Germans quit their long-range reaching for the bridge and we had quiet for a while. The ambulances came up to get our wounded whom we hadn't been able to evacuate, and when we brought the stretcher cases up, the civilians came out, too.

We saw her then and knew her beauty. Watching them, we gathered something of the story. Parts of it were plain enough to us.

Jack was helping carry Harley. When we maneuvered to turn the stretcher on the landing, she was in our way and stepped back into the corner of the staircase. She didn't look at us or speak but, as the kid went by, she reached out to lay her hand across his brow and smiled at him.

Except for her, the refugees were just an average lot, like others we had seen, all frightened and pitiful. We helped them all we could and they were grateful.

They were, as usual, mothers with young children and others who make up the flotsam and jetsam of war. There were old men and women, sometimes all alone. One could see the puzzlement in all of them. The women showed despair and covered it with the bustlings of the children. The old ones helped as best they could, but fussed the most about their backloads of possessions. As one pair of ancients climbed the stairs, the *grandmère* stumbled, blinded by the glare of the lowering sun. The woman who had beauty reached to help; she caught the old woman's arm and saved her from a fall. Instantly, the air was thick with chatter as the old one raged and yanked herself away. It was as though a leper had touched her arm. A peasant left her little charges to help the old folks and threw a single word. The woman only smiled. She did not flinch or turn her eyes away, except to throw a glance at us to see if we who listened understood. She knew she held our interest. She knew men.

Several of the fellows made tentative advances, poorly covering their interest in her womanliness, by treating her with the kindly friendship we all gave the refugees, but she would have none of them, answering, when she answered at all, curtly and in very good French. She was not cowed by anything that happened, and though one could see a stricken look of grief, she held herself above us all, maintaining her poise and asking no favors. She found a quiet corner of the courtyard where the moss-grown wall of the yard dropped sheer away to the town end of the bridge. She was a lonely figure: still-faced, motionless, watching a little river winding southward into France.

Soon the refugees were gone and one could see them walking down the valley, strung out along the road, leaving behind them the stark desolation of their town. The young and husky women with the older children disappeared first, around a distant bend, and last of all the ancients, stumbling on, with *grandmère*'s wicker carryall riding humpwise on her stooped, old shoulders, and *grandpère* following after with his barrow full of goods.

As evening drew down to the last of the sunset, the lonely woman left her chosen place. It was as though she had made a decision at long last about what to do, or else had waited for the end of the day to take to her road. She passed among us, her glance cutting through the few who met her eye, and made her way to the garden of the old château. We saw her stand awhile by the filled-in shell hole where we had put the German dead we'd found about the place. We watched her go down into the town and cross the little bridge. For a time we could see her solitary figure walking away into the protecting shadows of the coming night.

Piece—or Peace?

We had a quiet evening that third day. The refugees, the wounded, all had gone and left us holding forth at the château. A group of us stood by the courtyard wall and talked of things: the rifle companies, the sniper Gene had killed, why in hell they hadn't sent some food, what we would do in Paris some fine day—the usual things that idle soldiers talk about.

The girl who had been a German officer's companion had left a short time before and now made a lonely figure on the road below the town. Men's eyes followed her and conversation stopped. She had been safe with many men around, but every lad among us had his thoughts. It had been a long time since we had seen a lass like her. Some of us had lived a normal life at one time. We had a healthy hunger in our blood. One frankly speaking soldier spoke his mind, ending our reverie.

"Boy, was she nice! Christ, I wish I had a chance at that—"

"Been lovin' up these goddamn Boche, y'know."

"—an' did you see the way them Frog women hated her?"

"They say the women scalp her kind for givin' comfort to the enemy—"

"Did you say 'comfort,' soldier? Boy, she made me uncomfortable. Was she nice—!"

"Damn, I wish I could get a piece!"

Bud, the curly headed bellhop, wandered up. He hadn't heard much of the conversation, didn't understand the bit he caught.

"Peace? Did you say peace?"

165

His glance swept up the slope of the crowding hills to where the last of the sunset burned the sky.

"I'd gladly die, right now, guys, if I knew that it would give us peace."

The fellows didn't laugh. They loved the lad.

Have You Ever Heard—?

Have you ever heard an infantry battalion go singing toward the front under a summer moon? Or the golden tenor of a choirboy's voice breaking the muffled, marching silence of the road with the hunger-music of "There's a Long, Long Trail"? Or others picking it up all through the column 'til it rolls back to you in waves and waves of sound?

We were the young battalions. In the early days of our war, we were wont to sing. At least the replacements sang. We who had been there a time or two before didn't sing much. We left the singing to the golden boys with the golden voices—the kids who didn't know yet.

We remembered what Walt Whitman had said of our generation, "I hear America go singing to its destiny." We heard young Americans go singing toward the front under that summer's moon. We listened as they sang the marching songs; knew they were singing prayers.

As the marches dragged out into the small hours of the night, we began to tire. We quieted and, sometimes for a long stretch, there would be no other sounds among a thousand marching men than the steady slap, slap, slap of feet on the metaled surface of the road, and the quiet rattle of equipment. At such times, always startling and amusing in spite of the weariness, someone would interrupt our musings by demanding in a tone of banter, "So and so, give us a regulation growl." And then, always to be depended on, one of our bitter ones would curse heartily and fill the air with the venom of his hate—and we would laugh.

We had a few like that. They were good comrades, good

167

soldiers, but bitter, cursing men who hated everything about the game, yet always went along with us to play the gamble out. It seemed that they were men who dared to think and to question the why of things.

We had a lad among us whom we loved because he was a kid and made us laugh. We all played big brother to him, though most of us were youngsters under twenty—he was that young. Many times I'd heard the fellows say they hoped he would get hit someday; just hard enough to get him out of there, away from the front. It was no place for him.

I had his story. It was the same for most of us except for age. He was too young. We didn't want to see him wasted, for he was one of our golden lads. We loved him.

His Michigan home had last seen him soon after the American drums got to rolling. He had lied about his age and got in somehow, and while his high school chums were looking forward to their junior year, he walked the roads of France and was our youngest man.

He had a kiddish, laughing way of jarring us upon the march, when we were tired and walking quiet, going up for one more fight. There was always just one more until you fell. After that it didn't matter.

It was a silly thing and one can't put it onto paper as he gave it to us then, but it served a purpose, for he interrupted many bitter thoughts to make us laugh.

After he was wounded up near Jaulny, and we were coming away from there, I heard a hard, old gyrene sergeant say, "I miss that kid named Harley. I'd like to hear him yell 'how–de–dow' tonight and make the fellows laugh."

That Damned Shavetail

We came out of Saint-Mihiel in very good shape. We older ones knew that the army's 9th and 23d regiments had carried the load. We had just followed along in reserve. Our two regiments of regulars had, in less than twelve hours, carried out an operation that had been scheduled to take two full days. They not only reached their objectives but kept going, overrunning ours, too, in full stride. I remember that we once went more than four kilometers and only lost one man to a stray shell.

Our replacements had been shot at in anger, which was all to the good. But they had not been shot at enough. They had not learned. They thought they had been in battle. The guys from Belleau Wood and Soissons knew better. This had been a walk-away affair, with the Germans carefully and craftily withdrawing on prearranged plans; just holding strong points long enough to get the bulk of their men and guns away.

That was the first and last time I ever saw horseplay and swaggering cockiness when coming away from the front. We had been rebuilt after Soissons, full-up with green replacements. Now, after an imitation scrap, the kids were poorer risks than before. They thought they were veterans.

Replacement? Hell, I had been one myself back in June, but that was now two real fights and that Pont-à-Mousson thing behind me. In three months, I had become one of the "old" ones, a surviving bastard called "Lucky," so named by the battalion. Now the kids would be harder than ever to soldier with. They had all the answers.

We bivouacked well back of the front and lay around in the woods while the division gathered itself into traveling order.

169

Discipline was the most lax I ever saw. The kids wandered all over the area, looking up friends and swapping tall tales. Parris Island was a long way behind them.

Lieutenant Gear?[1] Well, let's spell it the way it sounds. In Virginia, they probably spell it differently, but Gear will do. Cold-eyed and efficient he came among us and, officer-like, he snarled, "C'mon, let's police this place up. Looks like a bunch of Spics had took over. Get with it, soldiers. Crumb this place!"

We moved. He was so right. We had been slacking. Gear was no ninety-day wonder. He had even been on China Station way back when. He was the sort of officer men would follow anywhere.

As he walked away, one of the green corporals, visiting from a nearby company, said: "Goddamn shavetail bastard! Who in hell does he think—"

"Ringtail" Mason[2] stepped in close, quiet-like. "Wha'd y'say, soldier, about a bastard?"

"I called him a 'shavetail bastard,' bud, an' I meant it!"

The left hook, a beauty, traveled maybe eleven inches. It was a honey, right on the button. The lad sprawled and, groggy, tried to rise. Mason waited.

"What the hell's the matter with you, bud? I just don't like that damned shavetail's looks. I—"

"Listen, son, he's a damned shavetail, but he's ours—*our* shavetail, see? So don't go callin' him names around here, kid. He was our corporal at Belleau Wood."

---

1. Probably 2d Lt. Prentice S. Geer, a corporal at Belleau Wood who was cited in General Orders 40, Headquarters, 2d Division, AEF. He received the Distinguished Service Cross and the Navy Cross, as well as a Silver Star citation for "having become isolated when the enemy counterattacked his group, he courageously charged with a bayonet and, with the assistance of his comrades, captured a machine-gun crew and repulsed the attack at that point."
2. Sergeant William G. Mason.

Heartache

Villers-les-Nancy, one of the little towns of France along the way, lies south and east of the parent city of wartime fame. We used it once for billets. There was one home . . .

The division was consolidated into the territory adjacent to the Nancy railhead; on loan to the French Eighth Army, which had a tough nut to crack. We were awaiting General Gerard's orders to go up. He's the one that soldiers called "The Butcher."

Our replacement men were now well knit into our combat outfits. To kill time, we drilled and drilled and drilled.

At evening, in the only peace we knew, we gathered on the village doorsteps, with the womenfolk and the old, old men. There were children, too.

There was one home . . .

On one such night, a dozen of us were sitting around trying out our poor soldier French and feeling close to something distantly remembered. It was a large French family of daughters. Widows? Yes, and some who waited and had heard no word for a long time.

A brood of children ran about and played a bit. We remembered that, because French children during the war years did not seem to play.

We made few passes at the women, though not because we were too good. They were under the eyes of one whom we called *grandmère*. She watched us too, and soon got rid of any man who didn't keep his place. She had authority as well as age, a matriarch to be respected, and was a sort of understanding godmother to all of us.

We sat around and idly chattered at them and among ourselves, held by something that we did not understand. The raveled strands of "silken cords to safety" made fantastic pattern here, and we were glad to rest.

With dark the children came, tired out with play. The older ones went clopping off to bed.

The little ones? Well, what do little ones do? They cuddle and grow sleepy—and there were eager arms to hold them close.

There was a lad—a lad from home, back over the Atlantic. A quiet fellow, too, with cold blue eyes and an old face, still too young. We remember that he was mild and sweet, and he always had a puzzled, questioning expression. He often smiled. I never heard him laugh. He gathered in a child—how she liked it—and snuggled her tousled head of smoky curls in the shelter of his arm.

Time passed and conversation lagged and we were thinking. The chilly night closed down; some sought billets at the call of taps.

He borrowed a blouse to keep her warm and held her close—just to keep her.

All of us were busy, thinking things.

Came steps along the cobbled street and with them a voice of order. "All right now, you men, turn in," the sergeant said.

We stirred. The spell was broken. The sergeant drifted off—'twas time for our billets.

We said farewells. Old *grandmère* spoke and we surrendered the babes we held, though one of us was slow to move or hear.

He buried his face and kissed her; he made her whimper and again buried his face.

I thought I heard a sob.

Grandmère

Late September. There was a trace of frost on the cobblestones. Little wisps of mist curled along the surface of the water in the old stone trough.

Men, disheveled, bleary-eyed, and sleepy, came from the lofts, brushing chaff and straw from hair and uniforms.

You saw them shrug against the morning chill and slap their arms about to stir their blood. You watched them shed their woolen shirts and plunge arms and faces into the delicious water, to come up laughing, sputtering, and shake the icy drops along a comrade's back to make him wince. At such a time, there's always one or two who have to sing.

Some had come to France by way of England, had been for a time on embarkation duty there. They knew some Limey marching songs:

> Take me back to dear old Blighty
> Put me on a train for London town—

Or, imitating cockney language, wail:

> Good-byee—
> Don't cryee—
> Baby dear, wipe the tear
> From your eye—

"Pipe down, you men. Fall in!" shouted the sergeant.
The men formed ranks. Another day of war. Roll call.
There was a heady scent of coffee and bacon in the air.

173

Healthy, hungry men. They rolled their packs or sat about on curbs and doorsteps, cleaning rifles, passing jokes.

"What's the news from the 'head'?"

"Yep, heard it from a regimental runner."

"Just this one more fight, 'n then we go to rest camps, see?"

"Who said this was a *bonne* sector? Christ, man, we're going into the Champagne front from here."

"Well, after that, I heard—"

"Liberty in Paris. Sure, I got it straight from a sergeant of the 12th Field."

"Hey, Slim, grandma wants ya."

Old *grandmère*, beckoning; her little flock of daughters, children, smiling from the door. There was one home—

"Why didn't y'pay 'er las' night?"

"Now she wants her franc, Slim."

"Pipe down, you birds, you goddamn—"

Grandmère had a little crucifix hung on a piece of twine for Slim. Nothing would do but that she fasten it around his sunburned neck. She pulled his tallness down and tied it carefully, inside his shirt. Her wrinkled, old hands rested a moment on his face. "My son, you won't die—"

You can't make jokes about folks with faith like that.

PART V

October, Blanc-Mont

Seasick

It was hard to say just when day gave way to night. As the first of us passed through the ruins of Sommepy, the last faint light of evening was fading in the western sky, while overhead the great silvery disk of the moon grew golden as we watched.

An hour before, the Alpine Chasseurs had carried their attack into the twin line of trenches on the hill beyond the town. The last of the wounded were coming down and we flattened ourselves against the earthen walls of the communications trench to let the stretchers pass.

The trenches held the rancid smell of burned powder and raw earth. The dead that we tossed downhill behind the trench were new and soft—almost warm. They rolled or fell like loose-filled sacks, their arms and legs asprawl in grotesque attitudes.

At one point, a large shell had blown a steep-sided crater just outside the parados and blasted out a part of the trench wall, making a convenient place for disposal of the debris of battle. The fellows hurried through the trench with the bodies and, grunting, heaved them overside into the hole.

A squeamish lad of ours, new at the front, refused to help with policing up the place; he just stood aside in awe and watched men work. Once, under the hoarse-whispered curse of a sergeant, he essayed to lend a hand, gingerly holding to a booted foot, sickened by the feel of it. The lad seemed fascinated, standing aside from the blown-out wall of trench and staring downward to where the moon probed at the twisted mass of dead things.

Men have their way of making jokes, their ways of breaking men, of disciplining. As the last of the bodies were pitched into the pit, two husky lads grasped the squeamish fellow from behind, lifted him face down and swung him, pitching him headlong into the yawning hole. His hoarse scream was muffled quickly as he fell. As he clawed his way frantically up the steep slope and into the trench, a noncom grabbed him and slapped him suddenly and hard to still his babbling.

"Quiet there, y'punk! What the hell's the matter? Did ya fall in?"

"Quiet there! What's up? What's all the noise?" It was Lieutenant Gear, his voice an angry threat.

"Dunno, Lieutenant, guess the kid fell in the hole with the stiffs. Scared him."

"Damnit, Sergeant, keep the man quiet, can't you? There's Germans in that trench right over there—"

A Maxim yapped and rapped, questioning. A great, bright flare arced up and blinded us. We stood in frozen poise and held our breath. The light sputtered down into the waste of no-man's-land, dimmed, and suddenly went out. Relaxed, we dared to move and breathe again. The lieutenant hurried off along the trench.

The lad staggered to a patch of shadow, hid from the moon by a bend in the trench, and retched violently.

There came a muffled laugh, a chuckling, questioning voice. "Seasick, son?"

The men were quiet, resting after toil.

Harvest Moon

A beautiful night. The moon was a golden washtub in a sea of luminous blue. A hidden radiance beyond the universe outlined both moon and stars and made a faintly glowing frame behind the sky.

Far above, so far they made but a half-heard whispering, the long-range shells mumbled, sighed, and tumbled through the night. Big ones, those. Fellows called them "seabags" and talked to them.

"Go way, way back, old shell. Don't come here."

"Go get them slackers, baby, those goddamn politicians in the Service of Supply."

"I hope that one kills that damn crown prince."

They were the big ones, not meant for little men. Smaller, screaming shells would do for us. The big ones homed on distant, vital things, on targets of importance, just casually on men. Men didn't count.

The shells made a sound like distant trains along a mountainside—speeding, fading, whistling silence into the distance. The nearby noises of the front would sometimes interrupt.

"Nope, kid, y'can't see 'em. Y'never see the one that gets ya, either. Now pipe down, recruits. Get some rest—"

Impossible to see, of course. Still, as you lay with your pals on the floor of a trench and tried to keep from thinking of tomorrow, you searched the skies. You found yourself peering, looking, picturing them like wild geese, and thought to see them pass in flight across the moon. And then your thoughts went back to home and harvest time.

There was mist down in the valley by Sommepy and on the

dead, old Champagne battlefield off to our rear. Here, high above the valley floor, we lay at ease. It was clear and not too cool. A blanket wrapped about the shoulders was enough. The trench was deep and wide and quiet. Talk was low. Palm-hid cigarets made dimly ruddy fireflies in the dark. There were dugouts near at hand. Deep and snug, where a man felt safe until he remembered. A single shell could seal the stairs and smother you way underground. It was better to lay there and look at the sky and take your chances in the open, to smoke and think and hope, and try to keep from thinking.[1]

Tomorrow. A full two miles away was Blanc-Mont ridge, a low, squat hill. The Germans had it now, had held the place for four long years.

"Will it be theirs or ours tomorrow night?"

"Oh, damn tomorrow! Anyway, my luck is good—I hope. Or is it time—?"

"That's sure a pretty moon. Reminds me of once—was it only last year?—the girl and me, with our bunch from school, were at Watson's farm. It was like this, the moon I mean. We had doughnuts and cider on Watty's porch that night, and sang old songs.

"Seems I remember someone wrote that Watty is in the Tanks now. Damn suicide outfit, that. I'll take a Springfield and a trench for mine. Seems to be the only thing I know.

"The girls were somewhat quiet and sad that night. Roy and Matt had both enlisted. Made a fellow feel guilty as hell, too—like a slacker—even if only eighteen.

---

1. Mackin tells on the tapes how he and Jack refused to go underground. They preferred to remain under other cover—even in the worst bombardments. He tells of a buddy insisting that the two of them come into a dugout occupied by three marines. They didn't, and a shell blew up the cellar-dwellers.

"Nope, the girls didn't say much. Just had a funny way of lookin' at ya, wonderin'—

"Wonder if the folks still got my dog? S'pose my kid brother claims it now—darn kid—always did want a dog of his own. My kid brother—

"Christ, I hope he never hasta' see a game like this.

"What? Did I speak? Hell, no—you damn recruits are always hearin' things."

We were runners, signalmen, a group of scouts, the officers, some engineers, and some recruits. We had a date on Blanc-Mont ridge—tomorrow. A thousand men were looking at the moon.

"Thanks, son, I'll take a cigaret. Why don't you sleep? Our damn barrage will start soon. Best get some rest.

"Bad? Naw! Hell, kid, a place like that is soup for us.

"Gee, I shoulda' sent the girl, the folks a line. I haven't wrote to 'em since back in August, and here it is October. Harvest time."

In a Fog

The officers would often tell us of the battle plans along our part of the front, but this day all were helpless for a time— except we knew the crest of ridge above was our objective.

A day and night of action, shifting here and there, had left communications in a sorry state. Because we had moved forward in the night, relieving other outfits, advanced along the rising ground under cover of fog and darkness, we were on terrain that was strange to us. A thinly clad, brushy slope fell gently below the German firing line.

The damp cold of that dark October morning chilled our bones.[1] Hunger pangs of more than forty active hours dulled our resistance. Men lay about in huddled groups in mounds of dew-wet blankets, keeping warm. We had not thought to sleep at all, but animal heat, soaked in from blanketmates, and weariness, put most of us to dozing. Sometimes a fellow's thoughts in such a place will make for dreams.

Our four had held together through the night and bedded down in such a way against the chill. We knew that, from time to time, others spread their blankets nearby and crawled in close to share our heated place. So, in company of other men, we four who had a memory of Hill 142 and other places shared, took our last bivouac in comradeship, together.

* * *

---

1. The bloodiest day of the war for the 2d Division in World War I, 4 October 1918.

"Runners! Runners! Get some runners here!"

The major's voice broke into our dreams as shells passing close overhead to break along the crest of hill had failed to do.

"Here, two of you—work left along our line and find the captains. Tell them—"

Our guns were pounding now, and everywhere was noise and shouting, heard between the bursts. Dawn had found us with ample work to do. No word of zero hour had come from regiment, no order to advance.

"Tell them when our barrage lifts to follow it—attack the hill!" the major shouted.

There were no men in close-piled blankets now. They stood about and shivered in the gray-lit fog, peering by habit upward at the line of fire; peeking with a sort of dread from beneath their helmet rims.

What do men think about at such a time? Food. How good those blankets were. And casually, sometimes, is my number up today? Is this the place I've waited for? There is no staring fear that anyone may see, except among the new men, here and there. Older fellows have an eye for signs like that. They keep watch and move them with a terse word of command; most anything will do, however pointless.

Why no word from regiment or brigade? Had a runner missed us somehow in the fog? Or had a long-range German shell found a more important target at a crossroad farther back? Common soldiers, our kind, never get to know the why of things. We only have the pictures from our memories, and what the politicians tell us—afterward.

183

"Hit, Gene? Are Y'Hit?"

The barrage caught us flat, crouched down along the slope below the crest and, for a bloody while, our losses passed all reason as we waited there for word of a zero hour that never came. The men were stunned; lashed down to earth by flailing whips of shrapnel, gas, and heavy stuff that came as drumfire, killing them. There was no place in all our little world for us to go. The fellows bunched against the fancied shelter of the larger trees in little close-packed knots, like storm-swept sheep, and died that way, in groups.

Experienced in places such as that, Gene, Jack, and Slim lay out in open ground, close-hugged in the cover of a shallow hole that reeked of high explosive. It's safer thus, unless your number happens to come up.

Bud had left us earlier, in running flight, to get a message back to regiment.

A large shell crashed some distance out ahead and opened up a smoking pit that offered sanctuary. Anything, it seemed, was better than the place we had. We planned to make a sudden dash for it, but held our spot throughout the tail lash of the storm, which slackened, passing overhead toward our reserves.

The last vicious shrapnel whipped along our slope of hill and a shell broke closeby. We ducked—cowering below its jarring power—held close an awful breath. There was a wrenching, sudden twist, a smothered groan; the sound a fellow makes when iron goes into him and shocks him, stunning.

—and instantly, alarm.

"Hit, Gene? Are y'hit?"

"Hell, no!" That sweet, low-cadenced, calm Missouri drawl was reassuring. A chunk of flying mud had jarred him, maybe? God, that was close!

We heard him say "Just watch that goddamn gas shell, the one smoking over there—"

The poison liquid, open to the air, was boiling up in yellow-greenish smoke that flattened over the ground, creeping, thinning out into killing stuff you couldn't see. The damp, fogged, breezeless dawn gave us space to watch it then, in safety for a time.

Then came the word to go. We ran; all of us but Gene. When we looked back, we saw that our old Missouri mule lay where he was; he hadn't moved. Running back, we knew; we knew damned well that Clevenger was hit. A chunk of casing had torn its way through his buttocks muscle and broken a hip. We bandaged him and thought of places back along the road that we had come together. We knew he wouldn't march erect again; kept the picture of his stoic mountain face and knew he'd never climb his Ozark hills. The stretcher bearers carried him away.

Four of a kind. Three Irish and an Ozark mountaineer. The hand was down to three, cold aces now—if Bud was anywhere around enjoying good health. Throw in your chips. Let's gamble for the pot. The cards can't always run a single way.

High spade? We'll take that bet! Go on and deal. . . .

"Ma!"

He followed the crown of the road, a strong and knowing youth who did not tramp the ditches as wiser men were wont to do. He was young and desperately anxious to hold his place in the ranks of hard-bitten men who played a wicked, vicious game. Boy-like, he wanted a place among them; sought their recognition. A little group of two or three untried men, new to the front like him, followed closely at his heel, half fearful of the risks they took. They tried to cover their nervousness and lack of proper training with a sneering, cocky smile at men who hugged the earth and stayed down low along the road.

Here was leadership in youth: green, untried, not yet fully feathered; just a spirit that said to the men around him, "Follow me!" Officer material? Yes, had he had time and luck and some of living. He was the type who leads a desperate charge and cannot tell you why—he just leads. His manhood ordered it so.

And there the shell burst got him, fully erect, walking purposefully along a smoky ridge in France. There was a reeking flash, a swift, sharp detonation; he sprawled, half pillowed on the shoulder of the road. Things were passing quickly. There was surprise and shock and wonderment and a bit of boyhood groping back.

He half spoke, forcing his voice, and said aloud, "Ma!" The strength to speak was not fully there. In the instant left to him came realization, and he said good-bye to life in high-pitched tribute, forced to speak out the thought closest to his dying heart. He screamed it loudly—just once—"Ma-a-a!"

"The Box"

Men seldom run headlong during an attack. There is too much equipment to carry for one thing, and you'll be out of wind when you reach your objective. That's just when you need it most if there's bayonet work to do. Sometimes the excitement, the lust for action, gets the better of judgment and you travel too fast, overrunning objectives. This is especially true if human game breaks into view to lure you on when almost all your officers are down.

The thin-manned wave that swept across the crest of Blanc-Mont ridge had expected resistance in the trench and hadn't found it. The fury of their rush, coupled with the sight of running quarry, led them on. The way led down a gentle open slope; the hunting was good. So they followed after. Momentum carried them to the foot of the slope and across a narrow, stubbled field to where resistance formed around a battery of field guns in a grove. Scarcely pausing, they shot the gunners down amidst their pieces and chased the survivors into the cover of the patch of wood beyond. They were in their element—the Yankee style of fighting amid the trees.

The line broke into scattered groups, all pressing forward. Working so, in vicious little deadly packs, they kept going. While the fever of the attack lasted, discipline was forgotten in the urge to hunt and kill.

When the officers who were still left could command the situation, the men had gone too far afield.

The wily German had drawn his troops away to either side as the hunters ran down their quarry and now Heinie had the remnant of a marine battalion bottled in a long, narrow belt of

187

woods, with the slope and stubbled field behind them. It was a place for men to die; a spearhead of out-flung battle line thrust deeply into the German front, exposed to fire from three sides, its line of communication cut off by enfilading Maxims firing from the flanks. It was a deadly place. With good reason did the hundred-odd survivors who came out of there name it in their memory "The Box."

Bayonet Lust

After the Alpine Chasseurs and other French units had cut their way across the plain from Somme-Suippe to Sommepy, and carried the fight to the ridge behind that town, the Americans took over. Days later, with French on either side to carry out the flanks, the last stages of the battle rolled in stubborn waves up the long, dun-colored slope to Blanc-Mont ridge, the key position of the entire defense along that line. Throughout the day on 3 October, two regiments of infantry and one of marines carried the attack up the bitter slope and even splashed its broken waves on the escarpment of the ridge itself. For four years, the old Boche had entrenched there and wanted badly to hold that place.

His orders were, we understood, "To hold—to hold at any cost"; and, like all troops of quality, he obeyed his orders.

In the gloom and smoke and mists of night, the 5th Marines filtered through the battered ranks of their compatriots to take position on the foot of the slope and on the slope itself, to carry at bayonet point the cresting trenches that lay between them and the final winning of the war-torn ridge.

The survivors of the army's 9th and 23d regiments and the 6th Marines slipped away and took cover in the nearby trenches below the hill, dug in, reformed, and tightened their belts to support the rush of the 5th Marines, should help be needed.

In turn, the 5th Marines—poised, restless, keyed-up to the breaking point—consolidated here and there. They mapped the road ahead in memory, taking for illumination the fitful light of a hunter's moon as it slipped from time to time from behind the clouds.

They dared almost too far it seemed, easing forward, taking advantage of the shelter offered by the scrubby pine and cedar along the battered slope, and cutting down by stealth the distance between a waiting enemy and themselves. It was almost as if they knew that when zero hour came, it would be short shrift for those who took too long to cross no-man's-land. Maxims can make such a mess of charging men.

Six o'clock, and zero somewhere out ahead. Who knew how long to wait?

There the counterbarrage caught them, massed along the slope, their own shells breaking on the crest, with no room for men to go and live in any numbers.

Feared and half-expected, the intensity of this drumfire baptism caught them unprepared and clear of any shelter.

What are minutes at a time such as that? What are hours? Who can measure passing time?

The battalion was dying where it lay along the slope. There was no way to cover up, no chance to get away. You could only lie and wait and take it, seeing the men around you writhe and die and suffer.

When was zero hour, the time to charge? We did not know.

A runner brought the word. "When the barrage lifts, go in and take them." There wasn't long to wait.

Did an officer blow his whistle? Was there any call or signal or command? We never knew.

In the murky smoke of that October dawn, men who could no longer stay heaved themselves to their feet and started forward. Most of the battalion did not go with them. But things like that do something to the souls of men. Those who live—they cannot run away—can only go on and make their bid. It was a thin, lean, hungry line of stalwarts—desperate, bleak-faced, and cold in fury—who charged the cresting trenches on the flame-drenched hill above.

190

The German broke. He couldn't wait. He couldn't stand and take it. Those who lived and could go on backed down on their reserves.

Objectives? A shallowed, blasted trench or two, flattened to nothing. And beyond, down a soft and gentle slope, was running game in view; the men of fury did not pause. Consolidating a hard-won point meant nothing here to the thin-manned line that did not hesitate, but followed, charging down. Resistance broke before it.

A lean young Yankee soldier carried on a crest of hysteria, fear, and a choking urge of exaltation, came down the slope and his quarry broke into a run. Two German men. Something of the fury of that cold, unstopped advance, coupled with the sight of comrades running rearward, told them to give up the fight. So they started back, intent only on rejoining their kind.

What is pursuit, and game, and the urge to conquer? What is there in the sight of running men that draws one on and whets the appetite with lust that knows no ease?

The beast was loosed. The thin veneer of civilization was scratched and broken, the caveman in him revealed. It was a race—short, swift, and deadly—between two who ran in fear, and one who followed after in fearing passion.

Who is faster? Pursuer or pursued? Why did they stop? Why did he run them down?

The leader swung about and raised his arms in swift beseeching. Seeing this, his comrade turned short about and stopped to plead, but turned too late. A hip-flung bullet crashed into his body and knocked him backward. Then came the charge, blood-hungry now; a bayonet was buried in the body of a living man.

He wrenched to twist it clear, but fainting flesh held it fast. He shot it loose and paused to look, and then, late in dawning, came reason. Here were dead—his own kind, two of them— and he had not meant to do it.

The charging line swept by, but the fight for him was done.

There was something in his face, half-stricken, fearful. He turned questioning looks on the men who passed, as though he sought from them some vindication. His eyes were large and staring, and he had a silly, heartsick smile. He turned to follow, trudging behind the battle line in an effort to keep up with the attackers.

"Farewell, Bud—"

The width of the stubbled field had been easier to cross at the time of our attack, but now the Germans reached for it from either flank with Maxim guns. They had us trapped, and we holed up there for six full days and held the place until the 36th Division cut us loose in one wild charge.

The stubble footed out along the base of ridge where the enemy had been and gave the Boche an open view across the rear of our battalion. The major, watching from the ridge, our first objective, could picture how the fighting went. He saw our danger when the French did not support the flanks as had been planned. The place was dotted here and there with khaki figures sprawled in khaki grass and broken stems. Our runner group was nearly all in that one field.

Bud had made a full round-trip or two and so had Slim. The word for answer then was: "—ammunition, too; get us some help up here. For Christ's sake, hurry! Reach the major if you can—"

Slim paused to get his breath, flopping down among the little stand of cedars where the battery of 77s had stood among their crews and horses. Too late, they'd tried to sneak those guns away.

He surveyed the open field and dreaded it. It didn't look to be a healthy place.

But the major was waiting yonder on the ridge; it was time to go.

Someone came crashing into view, running rearward from the brush—the runner, Bud.

He gasped out, "Wait—get my breath—let's go together when we go."

There was a little time of waiting, weighing, seeing things you knew were there, yet couldn't see.

Bud led the way, a frenzied, fleeing rush that took them halfway across the field before the guns swung down.

"Oh, legs, stay with me"—he saw underbrush and cover ahead—those few, short yards to go. The air was full of cracking, keening things that whispered past, and one almost felt the breath of them.

Bud fell as trackmen fall—a dozen reaching, stumbling paces, in partial shelter at the edge of the field. Both men were down; they formed a quiet, huddled heap. The guns swung off and left them there. It takes fear-frozen nerves to play the 'possum trick at such a time. Pioneers and Indians—such folks as that made the game part of our heritage.

Bud? The bellhop out of Binghamton? The altar boy?

"Private McGraw, sir? Yes, he needs a stretcher. Got a couple of bullets in his spine."

Jacks or better? Or will we make the next round deuces wild? Bet or get out, fella. Deal the cards.

A Glittering Gem

The major's word had been, "Get out to the companies. Stop them. Tell the first captain you find to stop advancing and dig in. The battalion has already gone too far. The French haven't advanced on either side. We are walking into a trap. Get going *now*, find them and stop them!" Jack Fackey and I shoved off, moving fast. We had been across the wheat stubble before, but not deep into the scrubby woodland where the battalion had gone.

That was where and how we first found the German engineer camp with dead horses and dead men sprawled amid the hutments and the slit trenches. That place was new to us. A place and type of living we hadn't seen before. We saw the dead. We noticed a wounded man or two, but we were making knots; there was no time to look about or loot or help with anything.

Beside a graveled path, toppled across a knee-high bit of fence, a half-dressed German lieutenant lay fresh-killed. I noted his out-flung left hand, palm down along a bit of flowering growth. I noted the brilliance of his finger ring, gleaming, dancing bits of morning sun, a glitter of gemstone amid the glowing gold.

Jack had found a path off to my right, a road of sorts, between the hutments and the stables. He was somewhat ahead of me, hurrying, glancing keenly here and there, seeing everything that moved at all—and many things that didn't. We couldn't be sure all the Germans had gone; there were always liable to be some.

One German, an enlisted man, probably an orderly, broke

cover ahead of Jack, scooting across the roadway like a frightened rabbit, letting fly a hurried pistol shot as he sought the shelter of a smashed baggage wagon. Jack fired in return and missed, something he did not often do. But then, both men were startled at seeing a living enemy so close at hand. The German ran, ducking and dodging through the scrubby trees and underbrush, wasting poorly aimed shots at Jack, who tried to run him down. Man to man; they saw only each other.

Movement. Ahead of me a figure moved and paused and took his time to carefully aim a heavy Mauser pistol at Jack, intent on killing him. I was safe—unseen and well within pistol range—along the stretch of graveled path. The German officer had paused on the steps of one of those beehive dugout stairs in full view from just above his knees.

I dropped him with my .45, the slug getting his shoulder point. He fell from sight, toppling down the stairs. Jack and the orderly exchanged final shots and the first German died. Running up the path, I took a glance at mine, huddled in a heap at the foot of the stairs. He wasn't moving, but knowing what a Colt can do at such short range, I didn't expect him to be.

We saw troops of ours ahead and we separated, trying to find someone to give the major's message to. I found my skipper, the captain of the 67th. He sent platoon runners to the other companies while I caught my breath.

"Now, can you get back?" the skipper asked. "Get to the major if you can an' tell him we need men an' ammunition. Heinie has begun stiffening up and he might counterattack at any time. We been pretty hard hit. I dunno how many we lost yet, but we need help. Get goin', *now!*"

When I got back to the engineer place, a machine-gun outfit, our 8th Company, what there were of them, had stopped to eat. They were sure getting some *bonne* souvenirs. In a drive like ours, the machine guns follow along. They don't travel with the first waves—they're too valuable, too vulnerable, too heavily laden for speed. They are the boys who consolidate a place and hold it. In a time of trouble they just stay there, and if things get bad enough, the infantry leaves them. That's why machine gunners are called suicide squads: they stay behind.

The 8th Company had found grub, the best of grub, and there was plenty for all of us. Beans, beautiful, simmering, smelly beans, rich with pork. My poor gut turned inside out at the smell of them. When had I eaten last? Well, you try to think back a day or two—or was it three?

Let's see now, we lost a day in front of Essen Trench because the division didn't all get into the lines. Was it on the third? The 9th and 23d Infantry and the 6th Marines went after the ridge, and we followed along for the main assault. That's right, and this is the morning of the fourth, and the outfit took the ridge with bayonets—Jesus, was that only four hours ago?

Now I remember. I split a can of hardtack and some corned beef with the guys up there above Sommepy, the night of the harvest moon, on the first of the month. Grub had been damn scarce since, but it always was when you were with the French army.

Filling my belly with beans, thinking about food, I remembered and I laughed. Sure, it was days before, on the first of the month when we were on the way up. We had hid along a sandy ridge watching the Alpine Chasseurs with borrowed glasses, as they pushed Heinie out of the old trench system and beyond Sommepy. There had been a Frog artillery outfit near us, heavy long-range stuff, and they had a small tent down in a hollow. Was it wrong to steal? Sure, but we were always hungry when we soldiered with the French. I got nominated to get into it while Clevenger guarded me. All I got was a few loaves of near-black bread, strung on a stick the way the French handled it, and onions—great, huge, mild things like the ones we call Bermudas.

It all happened so damned fast. As I rolled from under the rear wall, a Frog grabbed for me, just as "Mule" grabbed for him. Cleve knocked him cold. We both scooted away through the sand hills. Remembering, I quit my laughing. The Mule wouldn't be around to save me anymore.

We'd all been out with messages a time or two that morning, starting at first light, and the four aces, we four lucky runners, were together for a few minutes before the drumfire began.

Battle taught us things, not all quite true. For instance, soldiers along the western front honestly believed that shells never landed twice in one spot. The German guns had caught us flat and sure were raising hell. Jack, always our push-off guy, yelled and motioned. Ahead of us lay a battered, shallow length of trench, better cover than we had right then. The word was "Go." We ran.

Meanwhile, death was claiming our battalion. I've tried to remember. I asked among the men from time to time. No one ever seemed to know. Did someone blow the whistle? Did our barrage lift right then? Did someone yell? Damned if I know. I was so far behind the first wild wave I just couldn't tell. Never in my time had I seen such a deadly, killing fury.

The Germans died or fled. I do not remember then, nor for days afterward, any prisoners being taken. I just do not remember.

"By the way," I wanted to ask, "who among you dog-robbing machine gunners got that Heinie's diamond ring?" I should of, but hell, I didn't. The fellows used to say that robbing German dead don't count in heaven.

"Elephant Iron"

The curved and corrugated-steel buildings the navy built later became known as Quonset huts. I do not know what the Germans might have called the stuff used to build them, but our name for it was "Elephant Iron." And we found it in use by the enemy as early as October of 1918.

Back of and well down the slope behind Blanc-Mont, in what had been a cedar and pine seedling forest, German army engineers had been well dug in for years. Being engineers, able and well-supplied, they had one *bonne* sector all to themselves. They were still horse-drawn, as most all of us were then. Their stables and granaries were of rough-sawn lumber; their cozy little cottage-nooks were of better stuff. Like troops of quality, they had shelter trenches ringed about their camp—narrow, deep, and twisty, making them good for cover.

Best of all in way of protection were their Quonset-type dugouts. These were great square holes dug maybe six or seven feet into the earth and walled with heavy planks; they were like cellars of a sort. Over these holes they placed the great thick sheets of curved and corrugated Elephant Iron. Dirt from the excavation was spread on these, making for a bee-hive type of place with several feet of earth over it. Only a heavy shell could penetrate; stuff from light artillery just bored a hole in the sodded, grass-grown roofs and exploded, throwing dirt about and scarcely denting the iron.

Most were roomy, allowing for a table of sorts, a chair or two, even, in some, a small wood-burning stove to kill the chill of being underground. Almost invariably, each held bunks in double decks, wide and roomy enough to sleep four men on either level. I spent a night or two in one of them and when the heavy shells came searching for us, the shelter shook and jumped. Once, trying to bring my diary up to date, I wrote by candlelight and several times had to pick up my bottle candle-holder and relight the thing. Only a direct hit was figured dangerous.

Each hutment had its tiny space of yard, its flower bed or two. The walks were spaced and graveled, raked and clean. And every path, it seemed, had a border of rustic knee-high fence of curved and shaped cedar branches, intertwined and woven into patterns.

The Germans had been slow in moving out and our morning guns had caught them right at dawn—at breakfast time, before the men or horses had time to eat. Harnessed four-horse teams hitched to high-piled combat wagons lay sprawled in shell-torn death, a man or two among them amidst a rack of wheels and baggage goods. One fellow lay on his high-sprung driver's seat, his reins wrapped tight about his hands, driving dead horses.

"Berta"

The German counterattack came just at dusk and appeared to be an attempt to cut off the company that held the farthest corner of The Box. After three days of battering and the attendant losses, the men were in poor shape to withstand it. There was a while when things looked very bad for them.

For the first time, panic had its way, and a few men ran as the attack closed in. Marines never retreat, but these, a handful anyway, just got up and left for other places under the cover of dusk. There wasn't time to tend to them. The firing line was too busy.

In the minds of those who stayed, their going settled things and fellows took their time to aim, knowing that they had to get their price in men before the assault wave swept over them. It was there that training counted: discipline and tradition. Some had lived through spots like that before and paid such a price in what they thought was selling out that somehow they won through. And so it was again.

The attack came in close, through all that cutting rifle fire, and someone began using grenades; that turned away the German tide.

Their leader was a big, blond Saxon. Until he fell, they had a chance. A grenade went off almost under his feet and a fragment caught him in the groin. It was remarkable that he wasn't cut to pieces, for a Mills grenade breaks into lots of chunks of killing stuff and has the power to wreck a squad at least. He was a lucky man in many ways. Some of the fellows ran out to finish smashing the Boche attack and, for some reason that we younger fellows didn't understand, they brought him in, wounded as he was. He was the only prisoner taken there—or should we say "accepted"?

Because his case was exceptional and somewhat puzzling to some of us, we gave him as much attention as we could and noted two things about his actions that we wondered at. He was given the best of care under the circumstances, and all the time the first-aid men were bandaging him, he kept repeating over and over, "Berta, Berta." I thought that in his suffering he was calling for his wife, a Bertha somewhere. He was middle-aged and plenty old enough to be a family man.

The other thing we noticed . . . the motion of his hand. In all his pain, he repeated one gesture again and again, whenever anyone was working over him. He would place his hand directly and deliberately, palm down on the top of his head, then lift and lower it several times.

During the night, a two-wheeled German cart drawn by a captured mule came up with the rations. Our prisoner, lashed on a stretcher and wrapped in blankets, was loaded into it feet first. The stretcher was too long to fit the body of the cart, so it stuck out behind. Our last view of the wounded German was his head and shoulders protruding beyond the tailgate, between the stretcher shafts. One arm was free and with it he repeatedly placed his hand on the top of his head and mumbled, "Berta, Berta" over and over.

I didn't come to know what his gesturing and calling for Berta meant until years later, after the guns had ceased. When I received instructions in the secret work of a worldwide fraternal order, I recognized the hand motion the German had made in the black of a front-line trench lighted by the glow of star shells.

The Skipper Gets Wounded

The skipper made it a practice to travel well supplied with good cigars, and when things were hot we'd see him with a strong cheroot clamped in the corner of his mouth, barking orders like the noncom he had been in other days.

Walking but a few steps away, I was with him when he first was hit. He had just finished saying, "Bring a Hotchkiss over here."

The bullet caught him in the muscles of his neck and scarcely made him stagger. I swear he didn't even stop puffing on that big old black cigar. He stood there flat-footed and serene, as though it were a matter of everyday occurrence, while the rest of us sought shelter. He reached up to unsnap the collar of his blouse, opened his shirt, and turned the collar down, thrusting an exploratory finger into the wound along the side of his neck. After a little prodding he flipped the blood from his fingertips and gingerly took apart his first-aid kit, then wrapped the bandage in it 'round and 'round his throat, reminding me of a man having difficulty with his necktie. Finishing that, he buttoned up his blouse again and went on being the skipper.

Following men like these is what makes tradition for the fighting men. In the Marine Corps, for the most part, we followed real soldiers. There are a few advantages in serving with the marines in time of trouble, most of them having to do with the type of men you soldier with and take orders from. The vast majority of our line officers came from the ranks. They understood the soldier kind because in their day, their time, they had worn the harness and felt the lash—the harness being the burden of the pack equipment carried, the lash being the harsh discipline meted out and the unquestioning response expected.

We didn't ordinarily have to soldier under the rich man's son for whom father or some handy politician wangled a commission on account of the family, although there were and are rich men's sons wearing the Marine Corps's forest green. But the man in the ranks has the advantage of knowing that, rich or poor, gentleman or otherwise, the man who leads him out to die, for the most part has a code of his own—a part of the tradition that says he shall not send men where he dares not go himself. The skipper and most of the officers I soldiered under were men who adhered strictly to that code.

Later that same day a bit of shrapnel hit him where it hurt a bit, in such a way as to bother him and interfere with sitting down. Neither of these wounds was serious, but according to all the rules of the game he should have gone immediately to the rear when first wounded. Now, with his second wound, and remaining very much the company commander, he made himself as comfortable as possible, lying on his side beneath a tree and trusting to his noncoms and runners to keep him posted as to the goings on of the day.

When morning came, he was still on duty and suffering— and not only from his hurts. He had a small pad and on it, sheet by sheet, was entering the names of men gone down in action. I watched him grow older as he wrote.

Later that day a shell exploded near him and a fragment penetrated the muscles at the back of his shoulder and he lost a lot of blood. After getting bandaged he proceeded to make himself comfortable again, insofar as possible, showing no intention of going to the rear.

A half-spent machine-gun bullet got the captain's runner through the fleshy portion of the thigh and seemed to break his nerve. He whined and cried and didn't take it as the other wounded lying nearby were trying to do.

It is probable that the skipper's nerves were worn somewhat

thin by then, because in all his pain he fished around and took a bar of chocolate from his pack and tossed it over to the wounded runner, saying, "Here, son, suck on this. Maybe it will stop your damn noise."

At about the same time, stretcher bearers showed up at the captain's side. These were escorted by Lieutenant Gear, the second in command. On seeing them, the skipper said, "I'll not be hauled away on that damned thing, Lieutenant."

I shall always remember Gear's reply. "I'm running this show now," he said. "You can't fight this whole damn war alone. Now, climb on that stretcher or I'll throw you on. You're going out!"

Resignedly, with the grimness of the grim, the skipper crawled aboard the stretcher and the twenty-odd of us who were left of his old company felt lost and left alone.

Mail Call

The battalion had come back from Blanc-Mont ridge. No, the battalion was still up there. But anyway, oh hell, let me get this straight. A hundred and thirty-four of us had come back from Blanc-Mont ridge. We had gone up a full-strength battalion, a thousand strong.

The men were shocked and dazed and walked about with queer expressions. Sentences stopped in midair as an individual scanned figures approaching through the distant trees. One saw expectancy, an eagerness of welcome, die on a stricken face. It wasn't him. He wasn't there. He was still up on the ridge.

There is no look so full of blank despair as that of dead hope, of the dead love of a man for a man—for men love each other in a way women cannot ever understand. Soldiers call it "comradeship."

The mail truck came with sixteen bulging bags of words from home. Why does the mail always come after a battle? So many times it is too late for whoever is still up on some ridge.

The runner group took charge. Blankets were spread on the autumn ground and the survivors stood about in circles, waiting. The bags spilled out packs of dampish stuff and women's dreams. Each envelope smelled of ink and mold and memories.

"Bob B—? Oh, him? Yeah, bumped off down back of Vierzy. Mark it 'killed in action.' Say, that was in July, and here it is October."

The amount of unclaimed mail was appalling. For each shouted name there came an answer—curt, decisive, from men who knew. Wounded, gassed, killed in action, missing in action; the unclaimed missives were hastily marked according to the shouted reply that followed the reading of a soldier's name. They grew into an immense pile, to be returned to the folks back home.

Here and there a letter found someone eager and waiting. "Here! Here! Jesus! Gimme that. I didn't think I'd ever hear from home again!"

But the called-for letters were few and far between. When a battalion has gone through four hard fights, there are many missing voices. These men remembered, and remembered, too, that all had not gone out as soldiers go.

"Al Fletcher.[1] Who? Hell, I remember him." One saw a grin of some contempt—and appreciation, too. Some men who couldn't take it used their wits and got away. Al Fletcher—he took off his shirt and rolled in a bed of nettles. Told the doctor he was burned with gas and got an evacuation ticket, too. He won't be back.

"Harley Gay? Yeah, Sarge, went out of the Jaulny château on a stretcher." That kid had guts. Crawled a mile with a slug in his leg to bring a message in.

And from a southern college, a letter forwarded to Mr. Samuel M—, B.A. "Say, what in hell does 'B.A.' mean? Must've forgot his damn initials. Who said bad accident? Hell, he was just gassed. I saw him goin' out of Thiaucourt and he was coughin'."

"Here's one, a rain-washed blob of purple ink postmarked Cleveland. Can't read the name. Who here is from Cleveland? This yours, Grimes? Nope? Hey, gimme, Sarge, I got a hunch.

---

1. There is no "Al Fletcher" listed in the muster rolls. Mackin used an alias here for obvious reasons—as he did for many others.

Yours, Slim? Nope, but Woody Wilson's mother uses purple ink and lives in Cleveland. He lets me read her letters. 'Dear Soldier Black Sheep.' Yep, I'll bet it's his."

Yes, they read each other's letters. Men share treasured things when women aren't around.

"Gil Badrow." A hard voice said flatly, "Dead." A new word, that, from these hard men. "Dead." He had been caught rifling the pockets of the dead of his battalion. He was dead too, as a man or two could tell. There are some laws that must not be transgressed.

The packets had all been sorted.

Alfred "Woody" Wilson, returning from a trip to headquarters, came through the trees and he was seeking mail. Covering his eagerness as he always covered nervousness of hope and fear, with a drollery of apt expression.

"Any for me? Any letters for me, gang?"

For a moment no one answered as he pawed hastily through the unclaimed pile, still questioning.

"Here's one, Al. I thought it might be yours."

A rain-soaked letter changed hands, faced with a blob of purple ink and postmarked Cleveland. There was no question of ownership or recognition. Somehow we just knew. Taking it, he wandered off among the trees.

After bagging up the unclaimed mail, Slim wandered off among the trees, too, and came on Wilson standing, staring deadpan off ahead, just looking back and saying nothing. There was trouble in his comrade's eyes.

"Bad news, kid?" asked Slim.

Without a reply the letter changed hands again. Slim leafed through six rain-washed sheets of purplish stuff without one line decipherable. Why was the mail so often wet and late and welcome? So many times too late for whoever . . .

Wilson lay his face along his arm, braced against a tree, and said, "Oh, damn 'em! Damn 'em!"

"Really Bumped"

Back on the ridge, where gray-faced, thin-lipped men had charged uphill with bayonets against a steel storm, the 36th Division of the Oklahoma-Texas National Guard had come and taken over The Box, where most of our battalion lay about.

Today, the Guard was pushing Heinie back while we were resting, acting as reserves. They were green, untried troops who charged in reckless ignorance and won. They paid a price in taking Saint-Etienne.

The chatter began. "Yeah, Brown, I saw him get it in the guts—when he was bumped—"

"Direct hit wid' a shell—an 88, I guess."

"Hell, what of that? It was only a dud—now them two guys at the corner of that wall—we only found a foot and a leg of one of them."

"Yeah, them guys was really bumped—"

Cannon Fodder

Wind fought with rain and drove it, thin and cold, in sudden gusts that drenched the plodding column of men headed to the rear to get some rest. The men were quiet, patient, weary beasts who had done their best in storms of sterner stuff and somehow won. What mattered then the price that lay behind?

A battered, filthy, ragged crew; they did not look like soldiers. Beards—week-old, bristly growth ringed around thin-lipped, silent mouths—helped to frame weary eyes that had a glare of madness in their depths, or gazed out blankly, hiding warmth and any thought of hope.

The wind won out. The storm clouds first massed and threatened, then fled and let the wan October sun shine down. Spirits rose against the warmth of it and voices broke out in talk among the files. There was a place of shelter up ahead, billets, food, and, maybe, bottled stuff.

"The field kitchens?"

"Yes."

The regimental trains had passed this way. The slow kilometers gave way to marching feet. The thunder of the distant guns was just a rumble now where we had left a hard-won ridge—and many men.

A fast-stepping column moving on a main road crossed our way and we fell out of ranks to rest and watch them pass by.

They were tall, clean-cut fellows, walking rapidly toward the guns. A new division this, just off the ships—not long from home. Was there such a place? This was a sight to make a soldier glad, strong stalwart men who walked with eagerness. We had walked like that at one time. Was it in June?

Rough, ribald jokes. The passing column laughed at the sight of us.

"Hey, crumbs! Why don't you wash your dirty necks?"

"—call them soldiers, son? Why that's a bunch of tramps!"

"Why don't you get some uniforms—and use some soap?"

"What outfit's that, you dirty, lousy bums?"

They asked for it. We had answers by then for such as that.

"Hey, you—the loud-mouthed bastard over there. You'll make a handsome-looking corpse, tomorrow!"

One saw sudden dread spread over his face, below a sickly smile that masked his fear.

"—an' you, long, tall, an' noble; have you got two good legs?"

"You're damn well right I have, you—"

"Well, you won't have 'em for long. One of 'em will be gone when you come out."

It wasn't just the ones addressed who flinched. The effect of what was said went through the ranks and cut youthful banter short. Imagined pictures. It was as though a curse had been placed on them; a superstition, a sudden, awful vision of what awaited them up ahead. They were just lads who threw their youth at us, already old.

"Hey, Lieutenant, you're gonna get a bayonet in your guts—"

The silent column paced away toward the guns. We took to our own road and cursed beneath our breath.

211

October Autumn

Always, always, you knew a feeling of keen regret that was almost grief whenever you watched the new men, fresh off the boats, come into the Zone of Advance. They were so pitifully young, so green, so unprepared, so full of wonder and worry, acting out their little business of the war; hiding honest fear behind pretended confidence, behind dumb questionings. At times, they asked you only with their eyes as they hurried past, headed for the front.

The old legend about the invincibility of the German army had begun to fade. It faded fast when their irresistible force met an immovable something on the Paris-Metz highway in early June. It was then, when one lonely, deserted, surrounded regiment of the 3d Division formed a triangle of battalions, dug in, and rifle-shot the guts out of the Boche at the Second Marne, that the tide turned.[1]

By conservative military estimates, and they said Black Jack had told Wilson as much, we were into the European war with a timetable based on a four-year schedule. No one had dared to dream that the end would come in 1918. However, after mid-July, the picture, the thinking, the very atmosphere began to change. While no one ventured the hope of early peace, it was evident that the Germans were on the run. The important thing was to keep them reeling.

---

1. This was the 38th Infantry Regiment, nicknamed the "Rock of the Marne" for its courageous stand at Château-Thierry.

We hadn't yet come to "no prisoners, nor stopping to bandage your best friend"—but we were fast getting there. Some of our oldest "old-timers," measured in terms of time with the battalion as well as age, were hard-bit, bitter bastards, who did not need to shave—at least not often. We always had a battered and bitter handful who had long since lost all hope of ever going home. They talked at times with a twisted sneer, about "when I stop my fast one, wherever in hell I am, I hope it'll be quick an' in the shade."

We had been in the American First Army at Saint-Mihiel. Then, for the fourth time that summer, we were "loaned" to the French, to their Eighth Army, for the Blanc-Mont affair. Back under American command again, we noted a change in things. Everything was push, push, push: C'mon, bud, let's get on with the goddamn war, eh?

Old battles, old losses didn't matter any. We kept on getting men—more and more, greener and greener, so pitifully untrained, so unready for death. They averaged maybe four months in uniform.

The new army had another story to tell. Some few were less than two months away from their draft boards. Many had never even fired a practice shot. They did have a semblance of discipline, a commonness of uniform. There the resemblance to soldiers virtually stopped. Not only had few ever fired a military arm of any sort, there were even some who came to France carrying relics of the Spanish-American War, those outdated Krag-Jorgensen rifles from 1898.

Poker-faced, we stood at the roadside to watch another column of them pass. Some made bids for recognition with half-hearted smiles, a gesture now and then, sometimes a shouted word or a question about the road.

There is an old story of a new recruit asking a front-line man the question topmost in his mind. "Hey, Soldier, tell me, is it really as rough up there as we are told?"

The classic answer, "Yeah, they shot a man up there one day last week."

Infantry. They slogged along under the weight of heavy, useless packs. Following the rule, each man, in addition to the hundred rounds in his cartridge belt, carried at least two bandoliers, sixty bullets to a sling—sometimes three or four of them. They were called "Pershing's Walking Ammunition Train."

Infantry. They may call the infantry the "Queen of Battle," but replacements never look like anything of much account. You can't believe you ever looked like that at any time.

"Infantry, did you say, Sergeant? Infantry? Hell, man, that's just a column of warm meat going up to the front to be cooled."

PART VI

November, Meuse-Argonne

Benediction

Stacked rifles stood in well-dressed rows along the sides of the street. Heavy marching packs were piled in ordered heaps where squads had stood inspection. Bandoliers of ammunition crowned the piles or lay with cartridge belts and bayonet scabbards, near at hand.

Men lolled against the shop fronts, talking quietly or drifting aimlessly from group to group along the way in quest of news. There came a burst of laughter where comrades bunched around some lad who had a way of making people smile.

Our new replacements, all nervous eager fellows, sought to join in with the older men and hear the talk of places they had been. Their eyes were full of questioning and hope, and not a little dread. Lone individuals, pretending an interest in passing scenes, an unconcern, betrayed themselves by being startled when someone spoke. They made a quick return to the facts at hand and hid their thoughts behind the masks men learn to wear against the world.

The golden sun of late October settled down across the fertile plain and hid itself behind low, drifting clouds. It left a breathless beauty in the sky to ease the thoughts of men who watched it fade. The evening bells attracted us from where we strolled in close-knit comradeship along the village street.

Jack led me with his thoughts. There was not a spoken word between us then. We took our quiet way toward the bells and conversation fell away to nothingness. The church, an ugly pile of stone, squatted on its mossy foundations and brooded over the town. Frost-reddened ivy climbed its walls

217

and sheltered flocks of birds that screeched, chattered, and quarreled among themselves. Pigeons strutted on the belfry ledges or moved away in little flights as we went up the stone steps.

Someone yelled. "Hey, Jack! Wait up!"

We watched Bob stagger and scramble up the worn stone treads. He had a leering, drunken smile, ingratiating, hoping that the lad who waited there with me wouldn't scold too harshly when he spoke. "Lemme go in with ya, will ya, Jack?"

There was something pathetic in the way Bob asked, something boyish, guilty. Something appealing in his sodden face, his bleary, humble eyes—he asked only for tolerance, companionship.

"—found some, didn't you? You always do."

"Yeah, Jack. Found some, got me a canteen full. You wanna drink?"

Half hopefully Bob fumbled at the snap of the canteen cover, then stopped when Jack dropped an arm around his shoulders, smiled, and said, "Yes, you can come."

We went through an ancient door into another world, a place of peace and of deep, quiet beauty.

The late sun streamed in, its vivid, heavy beams filtered through old stained glass, cutting slanting paths of dust motes down the gloom. There was a glow of candles far ahead.

No one spoke. We stood quietly inside the door and felt the restful silence of the place. Bob stood straight and square. He made a picture, standing with his worn, old helmet in his hands, staring up at the figures in the glowing windows. If either fellow prayed, it was inside.

After a bit, we slunk out quietly on tiptoe, conscious that we had intruded on a holy sort of place not meant for us. Bob shook off our hands as we tried to guide him down. At street level, he turned to face the church and stood there for a time studying it, as though he were storing up a memory. We saw him grin, a leering, twisted expression, and then salute before he turned away.

"You guys wanna drink? I'm havin' one."

The trucks had come. There was a bustle as men fell into ranks and began counting off. The noncoms ran their eyes along the files to see if any man had slipped away. Men did sometimes, when we were going to the front.

It was the last time up for Bob and many other men. The sun went down. We saw some stars.

Rumors

We left the trucks at Sainte-Menehould and followed a winding, climbing road up into the tree-clad hills of the lower Argonne. There had been very little rain for some time and an early frost had had a chance to work its magic in the trees. Men said it was the most beautiful autumn they could remember. You watched them grab at vivid-colored leaves that drifted by or kick their way through windblown piles along the roads the way children do.

We hiked northward by easy stages for the first day or two and watched the country change from heavy forest growth of mighty trees to scrubby tangled stuff all full of brush. There were places where the leaves had blown into piles among the rusty barbed wire by the road, or filled an old trench the tide of war had passed. The nights were snappy, cold. It was good to spread your blankets in the leaves and snuggle down below the weathered parapets, away from the cutting wind. You thought with gratitude of the men who had dug the old shelters and wondered how they were. You wondered if this was your last trip to the front—or if you would finally get it.

Another rumor had come through the ranks and left a disturbing thought. When the new men (replacements always seemed to believe everything) asked you about this Armistice talk, you scoffed at them. Old-timers knew there wasn't such a thing. Still, you fell asleep wondering.

All the talk of peace, of Armistice, began with McGuire.[1]

---

1. Corporal Brutus C. McGuire.

He'd heard it from a regiment of National Guardsmen just up from the railhead.

You saw men take a deep, full breath at the thought of it. You watched them look away beyond the front and picture hope. You watched men curl their lips in bitter disbelief, remembering the promises of rest camps, winter quarters, and other things. You heard them curse disgustedly at men who dared to dream, and call them fools.

Baldy's Browning

The voices rose to a furious quarreling. Instinctively we cocked our ears and sidled through the stand of brush to see. In our outfit, men didn't quarrel a great deal. There was a sort of unwritten tradition that didn't allow it. Men differed, yes, often and pointedly, but the rules we soldiered by demanded action of the direct and positive kind. In a clash of wills, fists usually flew faster than words, and differences were settled hurriedly.

Hawkins, a line sergeant, was one of them.[1] He was young, a good soldier, too, from over Texas way. But he hadn't yet attained that authority of voice by which the old-timers ruled us with calm, emotionless commands.

The other man was Baldy. That in itself was an explanation of why the altercation hadn't ended in the usual way. It had been tried before us by bigger, tougher men and hadn't worked too well. Baldy was an individual. We had a few of them. Soldiers' soldier that he was, he had never quite allowed the system of discipline to reduce him to the common factor of the ranks. He was an unusual character in that he had rights, both personal and private, and so stood out among us because he made them stick. That's not a common thing in soldiering.

The Brownings[2] had arrived, and swell tools, too, as anyone could see. They still rate with the best among the trade. And

1. Sergeant Charles G. Hawkins, Silver Star citation.
2. Browning automatic rifles (BARs).

Baldy felt he had a right to one. He had inherited a Chauchat in the wheat below Soissons and carried it a long and dreadful way. It had been an unlucky gun before he got it, and somehow he had worn away the jinx.

A deadly thing, the Chauchat. The men who had to carry them well knew. They drew attention and attracted shells, especially at night. When fired on automatic, the flash hiders did not suffice to dim the light they made, and the orange color of it helped Heinie locate them.

Here in the upper Argonne we were to trade in the borrowed weapons for up-to-date equipment. With the war near its end, it was high time.

The new Brownings. We had heard of them before. They had become—like so many other promised things—legendary. We had always known, it seemed, that someday they would come—like the planes to blacken the sky and put out the eyes of the German army.

Who knew? A miracle was before us in the form of those guns. The planes might come on the morrow.

Here was a new tool; they looked efficient, too. And, like boys, each gun crew wanted one. It seemed there weren't enough—there never was of many things—and Baldy took the only way he knew to get his due. His claim was just. He really was a gunner, one who had proved dependable and true. But Hawkins's disposition had been made.

The argument ended with Baldy doing the unheard of, going over all the heads of the lesser men to the captain himself, our new commander, demanding (there is no other word for it) and somehow winning his way.[1]

Later, we found Baldy at his best, in relaxation, sitting Indian-wise before his oiling kit and indulging in what was to

---

1. Captain Harry K. Cochran, KIA 1 November 1918.

223

him a sacred rite. Like a musician, he fondled, weighed, and shifted his new instrument of death. He would pause and peer, then brush away a little speck of unseen dust.

We had to watch. He wouldn't let us touch it. He was a craftsman and we were only troops.

Some men really learned to love that war.

Old Charles P.

From dark ravines, from ruined barns, from brush-grown fields where we had hid, the battalions of the Marine Brigade marched in single file among the ridges of the upper Argonne. We came in squad columns to hunker down where clean-boled beeches climbed a slope of hill to view a terrace nature made to form a stage. Miles to the north of us, the front lines rolled and muttered at the day, stirring restlessly toward a coming night, against a final drive to end the war.

An army general came on a beautiful black horse and lectured us; telling combat men about the lay of land ahead; telling men about a job to do along a route he'd mapped to reach the Meuse.

He talked bare-headed, his two-starred helmet hanging from a saddletie, his gloves tucked neatly in his Sam Browne belt. His riding crop, like his horse, was big and black and strong. He aimed it like a pointer, stressing things he wanted done, or slapped his booted leg to make a point. We gave him our full attention. He did not mince his words. He made us understand.

"—you are the troops who taught the world how to take machine guns—"

Men sneered sideways under the brims of old tin hats and muttered low beneath their breath. They understood.

"—before you there are twenty kilometers of machine guns. Go and get them—"

Bitter memories showed in faces. Here were men who knew the story well. Some had lived it once or twice or more. They didn't like the picture, yet they would go again. Here, too, were lads who'd never heard a shell fired in anger until a recent yesterday, and they had yet to learn to cringe at the yapping of a Maxim gun. Still in forest greens, just off the boats, they watched the old-timers, trying to figure out a fact or two.

We were the survivors of the Blanc-Mont "Box," our ranks filled out again with new replacements, reinforced this time by the famous Military Police Company out of Paris. Was it the 16th? Never before in action with the parent regiment?

"Way up there to the north is a railhead," continued the general. "Go cut it for me. And when you cut it, you will go hungry if you try to feed the prisoners you will take. You'll cut the crown prince's army square in two. It's the last railroad they hold this side of the Belgian frontier. Men, if you cut it soon enough, you may very well end this damned war!

"You'll bypass Landres-et-Saint-Georges. Keep outta there and never mind the goddamn souvenirs. Keep away from it because we're going to smother it with gas."

He pointed to our front and said, "Before you there are three low ridges. Behind the third, the German artillery is parked almost hub to hub. Go and get them! Don't let them take away a single gun!"

We pictured other places, remembered that the enemy artillery was always good. It often blocked the way. We thought of point-blank battery fire across the wheat fields at Soissons, remembered German men who stayed to fire and fire and fire across that stubbled field at Blanc-Mont, serving their guns 'til bullets cut them out.

"—now on those ridges all your officers may be down, but you keep going," said the general. "I want to sit back in my headquarters and hear that you carried all your objectives on time."

We remembered officers like that—had watched them fall, going up before us. They had a code to live and die by; to never send a fellow where they wouldn't go themselves. It was good to have soldiered with their kind.

"—and I repeat, on those first ridges, go forward while you

226

can still crawl. Top that third ridge and settle down to keep all of those guns from being moved. Do it with rifle fire if you have nothing else—you will be close to them."

And then he delivered his final punch, his closing line:

"—and now I say, and you remember this, on those three ridges, take no prisoners, nor should you stop to bandage your best friend."

For a while there was total silence. He studied us. We studied him. Finally, he raised his arm in something of a salute. His riding crop made an arc against the sky, a half-waved gesture of good luck, farewell. The black horse turned to trot away along a forest trail.

We moved quietly. File by file by file the battalions moved away, leaking stealthily in all directions, breaking up the concentration, going back to where our kitchens hid.

"Bastard!" a scarred buck sergeant said, talking half to himself. "Bastard, and he's gonna sit and watch our progress on a map, eh? Says he! An' where will we poor sonsabitches be? What in hell'd he call that place? *Kriemhilde Stellung?* Him an' his three ridges. The bastard!"

"Talkin' to me, son?" Grizzled Gunny "Johno" Johnston, his whiskers shot with gray, twinkled at the younger man. "Didn't y'like what he said, son? Now, there's a soldier, son. West Point stuff. I've heard've him. That's Summerall. Old Charles P. himself, from the First Army."[1]

---

1. Major General Charles P. Summerall, at the time commander of the AEF's V Corps. He arrived in France as a brigadier general in command of the 42d Division's artillery brigade. He was soon moved to the 1st Division, commanding the division artillery at Cantigny and the division itself at Soissons and Saint-Mihiel. He got his second star in late September 1918, concurrent with his posting to V Corps. He retired as a four-star general in 1930, after serving a four-year stint as army chief of staff.

Rest Camps

We slogged along through a night of rain. The general had lectured us two days before, now we were going up. It was a time for sober thinking. A seldom-spoken thought lay in the mind of every man, as always at such times as this. Is this my last time in? Is my number up tomorrow? You don't dare dwell too long on thoughts about yourself, nor dare to think of home— at least not long. If you're an old-timer of whatever age in this man's game, home is a place you've long since said farewell to—forever. It's easier to accept one's fate that way.

And your thoughts go out to the fellows around you, marching close at hand, and you wonder which of them, these pals and friends of yours, will die. Oh well, it doesn't matter. They are not important now, though you hope in your heart that a certain golden lad or two may yet be spared to go back and tell the story. None are important now. They never were. You only thought so at first. They only came to fill the places of the pals who went ahead, in the early days of this long, drawn-out campaign. And you wryly smile at the memory of some old-time pal who, like you, had once believed the story about rest camps and a liberty at Paris.

You knew the rest camps now. It was a standing joke among the columns. They dotted fields and forests and farmsteads here and there with rows and rows of little wooden crosses.

One Short Hour

"Pass the word," someone said. "Headquarters group to fall out here and let the outfit go on by."

They went on past and through us with a rapid swinging stride, each briefly holding silhouette against the battle light—to dim away into the zone of front-line action; to man the firing line. Runners reported back after a time, "Battalion is in position for assault."

There was a time of waiting. The barrage increased in tempo and the counter stuff came crashing back among us, searching for the locations of our guns. No walk-away this, as Saint-Mihiel had been. Here was strong resistance.[1]

Someone had said, "Hold them," and we had a job to do. It was to here that the Rainbow men had come and some still lay about, debris of battle.[2] Those left alive after we completed the relief went away from there, and they were making knots.

It was hell just waiting. Was it only one short hour? The earth beneath us trembled, jarred, and heaved about until men's stomachs retched from the shaking. Our guns were up among us, firing almost point-blank now, and we could trace a long flash-lighted slope in front, its crest alive with

---

1. The attack described here and in subsequent chapters was on 1 November 1918.
2. The 42d "Rainbow" Division. The nickname reflected the varied composition of this National Guard outfit, which drew upon twenty-six states and the District of Columbia for personnel.

colored flame. Somewhere near at hand, a shell crashed down among horses and a high-pitched screaming joined the chorus for a time.

Outlined against the glowing front came one lone figure, crouched and running fast. We were quick to question him, an automatic slamming muzzle-wise against his belt to make him talk.

Sometimes men leave, or try to leave on the eve of battle. It is a practice frowned upon among the trade. Two or three such ones may start a panic—we had a lot of untried men. It's orders to discourage movement toward the rear. But it was runner Lemons,[1] with a message for the major. He went with me, stumbling down a flight of dugout stairs. Then out again, from the muffled thunder of the dugout into the shrieking of the smoky, fog-strewn night. Midway to the front we old friends paused to bid adieu, lying in a shallowed place of battered trench and taking time to orient ourselves a bit—and giving thought, I guess, to other places.

Leaving, he crouched and gripped my shoulder, shaking me to make me understand, screaming in my ear, "Luck to you, kid." But luck for him was done. He got it as he wanted it, on his feet and moving. He hadn't time to think. He was dead.

I checked back with the major.

"His message? Yes—"

"'Twas so and so and so. Find the captain! Make it rapid now!"

The new captain,[2] a testy one and much a soldier, was lying forward of his line, down flat, full-stretched, exposed, and

---

1. Private Charles V. Lemons of Sugar Run, Pennsylvania, KIA 1 November 1918.
2. Cochran.

watching from a hump of shell-tossed sod as deadly fireflies danced atop a long, low ridge ahead.

Now to the front and this to be his first headlong assault. He watched and waited. Knew keenly then the place of leadership, its loneliness and strain. Waiting for his zero hour to lead a charging wave of men against a hill.

"Lemons? Dead, eh? Good man! Say, we've had a couple of dozen bumped just waiting to go up."

He paused and pointed to the front. "Those fireworks now, I've heard you had some pretty shows up here, but I didn't picture anything as great as this—"

Taking comfort from the shoutings of his voice against the thunder while the gray of dawn gave body to the mist and rolling smoke. There was an end of waiting. Was it only one short hour?

Almost lazily, the last few shells lobbed down along the crest of hill and someone blew a whistle in the fog. In the rolling mist of morning, against the fire-lit background of retreating night, the young men rose to their feet from out of hole and trench and dugout.

One caught glimpses of their young, set faces, stern and questioning, reluctant, too. They had a job to do.

Just before they moved away, a fan-fire of gun flashes threw them into vivid outline to make a picture for memory. Because their way lay upward, their heads were up, looking toward objectives on the crest. They were eager to go on up and get it over with. For an instant the firelight danced in living flame on a moving line of bayonet points.

Baldwin Dies

Here was the first of the general's three low ridges, the line of the front the Germans called the *Kriemhilde Stellung*.[1] The going wasn't quite as bad as we had expected. True, we lost some men, but we didn't know 'til then how good a job our guns had done.

We heard machine guns yammering, but they didn't sweep us as we expected them to do. There was resistance, some . . .

Musolf rolled away kicking, a sniper's bullet through his knee, and cursed a bit with a lurid impersonal flow of profanity, but we went on up and left him there.

Our orders were to "take no prisoners, nor stop to bandage your best friend."

We were two kinds of men: recruits and old-timers, and a lot of new recruits bunched up, as all replacements are inclined to do. They were learning, just as we once had to. They hadn't yet learned anything of lust, or hate, or pain. Beyond giving mass to the movement, they were but little better than spectators for the time, though we knew that within the hour the stronger man within each group would begin to

---

1. Known to the Allies as the Hindenburg Line. The division's objectives were the German positions in the Barricourt Heights, the last layer of the defensive belt the Germans had created in the Meuse-Argonne sector.

find himself and conquer fear, and start his bit of acting on his little part of the stage. The young ones learned that way.

Meanwhile, they picked an older leader near at hand and followed him, the other kind. That kind always leads the troops away to win or lose our battles and is copied by the less experienced men.

In action, youngsters curse these leading men, following them with heads ducked low and taking comfort from the mutter of their voices.

"If you can, damn you, so can I." They trail along, sustained by discipline, example, vanity, and much of pride. Tradition, that's the thing.

Because of slight resistance here, we had gone up a bit too fast. The slope topped out another couple hundred yards ahead and we took time to let the flanking waves come through. A whistle blew and we all took cover as it offered, or sprawled where we had stood and strove to map the road ahead.

There was no hurry. Men lit cigarets and smoked, drawing great deep breaths of comfort and giving their hands something to do.

Baldwin lay his nice, new Browning down, carefully placing it along two tufts of grass, and sauntered to a shell hole several yards away. He took his time and then stood, straightening up his clothes, peering all the while up the slope ahead, full standing in a line of sprawling men. He was a target then, and it seemed to me he didn't care too much. He long had known he wasn't going home.

He sauntered back, and then the whistle sounded and we rose up. Baldy, slightly forward of the rest of us, lifted his gun to drop the loop of strap across his shoulder and seated the butt in the cup along his belt before stepping away.

The sniper's bullet caught him full between the eyes as he was peering upward. He fell full length while striding forward up the slope and didn't move.

"Nor stop to bandage—" No matter, there was no need.

233

Harris, the first carrier in Baldy's crew, as was proper, got to him first and flipped him expertly. He lifted the loop of strap and freed it from Baldy's strong, warm fingers.

He stopped me with a look and shook his head twice, for I was closing in. There was nothing else to do. We kept on going. The new men watched and learned as we had learned before.

At the crest we found the Germans gone—all of them. Their two-line trench was a shattered ditch of earth. And we thanked our guns for the small price we had to pay.

Ahead lay one more ridge, and then another, objectives up ahead. There is always just one more.

Landres-et-Saint-Georges

Topping out on the first ridge we squad-columned across a waste of battered, twisted wire, and posts; the shell-torn, blasted ground where two German trenches had been a short time before. Trenches no more, they were shallowed depressions like wide, unkempt ditches with dugout entrances peering from the walls.

"For God's sake, fellows, will you look at that! Look at that goddamn town!"

It was and had been a walled village, like so many in that countryside, all built of stone. Now the village showed in little flashing glimpses under rolls of boiling smoke, a somewhat different smoke than what you'd think. This was greenish-yellow, shot with coils of writhing black, with now and then a glance of livid flame to light it all.

"There's the general's town. The one he told about, an' there's his gas. Look at that stuff boil, will you? Man! Nothing can live in that. Any Heinies that were in there when that stuff hit, strangled at once."

We watched awhile. There was no sign of life. No movement but the coiling deadly gas. It was a still, foggy morning with almost nothing in the way of breeze. The town just writhed and died within itself.

Gunny Johnston said, "'Member what old Charles P. told us? Nevuh mind the goddamn souvenirs!"

Down the slope we went, through a narrow, shallow valley, heading for another slope of hill. Somehow we were not a line of skirmishers anymore. We moved in knots and groups of men, sometimes moving in single file as we followed our leaders. The damned replacements kept on bunching up and had to be told off from time to time, and scattered out a bit.

Baldwin was dead. We'd left Musolf kicking like a stricken steer. Heddon had bled to death with both legs shattered into shreds of flesh and wool.[1] Many had died before the zero-hero whistle blew and others lay among the early slopes.

Looking back we saw lines and lines of men, flowing after us in endless waves, breasting over the crest of the first ridge, following after us as we faced the second hill. Always, always, we faced another hill.

Jack came sliding toward me at a jaunty left oblique, his Irish grin breaking up his face. "Hey, Slim, how about it? Do you want ham or bacon with your eggs this morning?"

---

1. Private Harvey P. Heddon of Brighton, Massachusetts, KIA on 1 November 1918.

An Officer Dies

Somewhere along the slope of the second ridge the skipper went down. Hudson Group, his company runner, went to him. It must have been a casual shot or piece of shell that got him. Certainly the bars of his captaincy hadn't drawn attention, for he had taken them off, as was common practice, and pinned them in the pocket of his shirt beneath a private's blouse.

He hadn't expected death, though he figured he might be wounded. A fellow had those hunches; however, sometimes they were wrong. He had jokingly told us once how he had provided for such things, and we knew he didn't plan to die.

"I'm going to wear my Sam Browne belt over my shirt under my uniform so that when I get hit and can't speak for myself, they'll know I am an officer," he had said.

While stationed in Paris, the skipper had visited wounded officers in the hospital there and knew, too, of the times they had while convalescing. He wanted to be sent directly there.

Group told us the last we were to know about the skipper, of how he had stopped and tried to lend him a hand. The captain had said, "Group, what were your orders? Get going now, damn you, and get those guns."

The guns were there, just as the general had promised. We topped out on the third low ridge about two hours after dawn. The Boche were trying to move some of the guns, and the fellows with rifles knocked down men and horses indiscriminately until all movement stopped.

After a time, the following battalion hopped off from there and went ahead to carry on the drive.

Group told his story about the captain and several men went back to care for him only to find him dead.

"Yah, You Missed Him"

The last battle of the last campaign was rolling across the three ridges back of Landres-et-Saint-Georges. The main line of the *Kriemhilde Stellung* lay an hour behind, no longer impregnable, a shambles of twin trenches. Formation had given way to trudging troops of combat units closing in on the last ridge, behind which the enemy artillery lay parked hub to hub. It was imperative that the guns be captured before the retreating Germans could take them along.

Somewhere back of the first waves, a support outfit was mopping up. Dugouts that looked too forbidding were given a dose of grenades as the hurrying men went along toward the last objective of the day.

A rifleman, slightly wounded up ahead, came herding back a group of prisoners for whom the war was over. At a point where the littered trail passed lengthwise of a stand of scrub, the leading prisoner, young and not too wise, bolted. Cutting back along the scrub, he was immediately out of sight of his guard. Freedom beckoned, and he ran straight and true to where his kind were in retreat. Caution, reason, and probably any conscious thought gave way to blind instinct of flight—of homing. By his own act he was sentenced to death. Such things just aren't done in good company, and the most generous spectator could expect nothing for the lad but that he be cut down. His startling act was performed in full view of a mopping-up detail, and within a hundred yards or so of men who were trained to kill at six hundred paces. Slung rifles leaped from the carry position and a split second of eternity intervened as an eager voice yelled, "I'll take him!" To men

238

who were weary of bitter deeds, the offer was welcome. Or was it the sporting instinct of the American bird hunter allowing first shot to him who kicks up the game?

A Springfield came to shoulder smoothly, easily, sights centered full and square on the back of the running man. In full sympathy with the gunner, all took deep breaths, then half-expelled them, awaiting the shock. No report came. The boy ran on. Nerves strained. The gunner moved and shifted, getting better aim. In silent protest at delay, a man or two half-lifted rifles to cut the runner down, yet paused to watch the denouement. Eternity was measured off by running feet.

An open trench yawned ahead and at full speed the leaping form took shelter. The rifle spat. A vicious spurt of death flicked muddy sod where last he had been in flight. Chagrined, the gunner turned with guilty face and said, "Aw, gee, I missed him."

Stares—blank, incredulous, accusing—and a soft voice drawled in generous contempt and understanding. "Yah, you missed him."

Somehow there was no note of censure. Faces lifted and the world looked bright against the sky. The objective lay ahead and the mop-up detail moved on.

Rain

The blowing, soaking, cold November rain began to fall while we lay on our objective above the ranks of German guns. As our excitement cooled and the heat of battle danger oozed away, the men grew chilled in the driving wet. When at last the whistles called us up to follow in reserve, we were glad of the chance to move. Once you get soaked through and used to it, it's not so bad except when you lie still awhile or stand in idleness where the cutting wind can reach your bones.

As usual, we were happy. We had been fed behind our lines the day before. We were too near the German guns for fires, so there had been no chance of good, hot food and steaming coffee. Instead, we had fared on canned corn beef and bread. Now all the strength of that was gone, leaving us with only our discipline and pride. We tightened up our belts and faced the front, plodding along patiently through mud and wet grass and dripping underbrush toward the yammering of guns that barked ahead.

Somewhere, the first night, we dug our foxholes along the rising slope of a hill, cutting away the matted grass and roots with our bayonets. You heard the fellows left and right of you along the line curse and growl and damn because the water seeped back into the little grave-like pits as fast as they removed the dripping gobs of earth. A fellow faces many questions then, among his thoughts. Do you wonder that some bitterness becomes a part of him, to mark and mold him for its own, through the rest of his days?

Picture men in such a place as that. Dark figures crouched on knees, their shoulders hunched, helmets hanging low across their eyes while a driving rain beats ceaselessly across their backs and drains in little rivulets from the exposed napes of their necks, to run down inside their collars in icy streams that cut against the sweaty warmth of their bodies.

The figures on the slope ahead were outlined by the livid flashes of the guns. To see them, hear them growl as they tear away at the earth like burrowing animals reminds you of mad beasts. It makes a picture that civilians never see.

Each man completed his firing pit, his shelter against fragments of shell, his little haven against the stray bits of death that reach from time to time for the reserves. Then, as each hole filled waist deep with icy water, he calmly rolled himself in his wet blanket on the open, spongy ground beside the hole, with his helmet serving as a shield against the rain.

It's remarkable how warm one can be at such a time and how restful such a sleep. The secret of it lies in being still. Your body heat, slowly penetrating through the thick wool of your clothing, warms the cloth that lies against the skin. The water in your blanket and your outer clothes forms a sort of insulation against the wind. Your feet, cased in sodden leather, are, of course, painfully cold at such a time. The rule is just to lie still. After a time, the feet grow numb, letting you fall off to sleep in drowsy comfort.

The most painful part of such a situation is the necessity of getting up to face another day. Even the balmy breeze of a June morning can feel cold then, whereas the steady knife-edge wind of November is pure agony. It drives inside to meet the chills deep in your bones and makes you shake. Your lower jaw trembles like a loose-hinged gate until you can lash it fast with your helmet strap, pulling your face together to stop the chatter of your teeth.

You see the men around you try to rise; see the pain in their faces as the sluggish blood tries to fight its way down to those dead extremities that are their feet. They first succeed in getting to their knees. They break out "makings," nursing the papers and little cotton sacks of precious tobacco close against their breasts to shelter them from the wind and wet. Somehow they succeed in making a cigaret of sorts, and fight against their numbed fingers to get a match to it. Ah, that first deep drag of burning smoke at such a time. You watch a fellow come awake then, instantly. His eyes light up with the ecstasy of pure enjoyment. Why is it that with that first deep lungful of smoke, a man can rise, all numbness driven from his legs and feet? Say, soldier, how would a good, big shot of cognac go now?

Beans

The battalion headquarters group held forth around a ruined farmhouse. The rifle companies had shelter in an orchard, hid behind the old stone walls and in the stand of woods around the place.

Big, long-range shells slammed in from time to time, to bite out parts of buildings, rip down trees, and kill a man or two each little while. Reserves are used to little things like that. Four of us were sent in a great hurry to meet one of the ration carts at a crossroads, a short distance to the rear, where each was issued a wooden case of pork and beans with word that they were for the major and his officers.

Coming back to the farm with our burdens on our shoulders, we stopped for breath along the slope below the orchard and took time to talk a bit and growl.

"Beans, for the officers only! What in hell are bucks like us supposed to keep a-goin' on?"

"Yeah! Yesterday it was we had a meal—"

"Call that a meal? A half-slice of bread, two little measly chunks of bacon, an' that lukewarm coffee? Christ—"

"—an' beans at that! Hell, all we guys get is canned tomatoes. I could eat three cans of those damn beans right now."

"—wish I had the guts. I'd bust one of these."

"For officers only! What a hell of a war this is. Them damn officers get to go out with the nurses behind the lines, have a dog robber to make their lousy beds and spread their blankets, draw a hell of a lot more pay then we poor bastards—and now beans, for them only—"

Whistles sounded shrilly up ahead. Van Galder, running

down the hill to hurry us, was shouting, yelling at our group to hurry up.

You saw men come to their feet along the hill, adjusting packs and grabbing their rifles where they leaned along the wall. You saw the waves of infantry form up and step away from sight along the crest. The slope was steep and we were weak and weary, feeling tired. The boxes cut our shoulders, weighed us down. The officers were somewhere out of sight.

The sergeant went his way, busy in the way that noncoms have. We heard him in the orchard, checking men.

In single file, we fought our way toward the wall. The last in line was having difficulty of a sort—his case of beans kept slipping, threatening to fall at every step. Directly ahead of him were men he knew, the blanketmates and comrades of the road. Almost at their feet, he stumbled, fell sprawling toward a pile of broken stone. The box struck cornerwise against a piece of masonry, a solid chunk.

Did he hurl it from him as he fell?

There was a sudden scramble, quickly ended. Fellows hurried away to join the little squad columns, stepping off, buttoning their blouses over bulging shirts.

Van Galder came through the gap in the wall and hurriedly kicked the broken box out of sight. We heard him yell: "Hey, guys, you divvy up!"

244

Morning in the Argonne

The front slept sullenly, with rolling, distant growls behind the slumber. Far off toward Sedan there was a deeper sound. A watchdog Maxim yapped from time to time, excitedly, in sharp staccato barks, to warn its master of the threat of dawn.

Men slept in cuddled warmth in mounds of rain-soaked woolly blankets, sharing body heat against November chills.

Morning came to the Argonne woods. The rain had stopped. The world was weirdly beautiful beneath a cloak of hoarfrost, clinging everywhere. Men, cozy-warm beneath the weight of their blankets, knowing comfort for the first time in many days, stirred restlessly against a sound of song.

It penetrated through a maze of troubled dreams and brought them up, half-sitting, wondering.

The golden tenor voice of a golden lad brought smiles to faces fresh from sleep. He lay in a frosty mound of covers singing:

> How warm I am
> How wet I am
> Nobodee seems
> To give a damn.

The sun broke clearly, suddenly, in full surprise.

Bitter Glee

We were only playing leapfrog. We had dropped along the crest of the third ridge above the ranks of German guns days before. Supporting waves took up the drive from there and carried on. After a time, we who had been the assault battalion had taken our place among the rolling waves of infantry and followed on.

Again—was it the third or fourth morning?—our turn had come to lead the drive. We hadn't had to fight so very much. The enemy had broken away before us, leaving scattered Maxims here and there to slow our advance. Their bravely desperate crews had done the best they could and died.

We never really understood such men. The crews were small, seldom more than two or three, and always young. The young ones stayed and died because their orders told them to. Older fellows would have used their heads—cried "*Kamerad*" before the guns grew hot and men grew coldly bitter.

This was the seventh morning.[1] We were lying in reserve, not far from the general's railroad. We heard increased firing up ahead and knew the enemy had stiffened up along the river.[2]

---

1. 7 November 1918. The 2d Division was exploiting its breakthrough of 1–2 November, keeping pressure on the withdrawing Germans.
2. The Meuse. The railroad mentioned is the line tracing the river's west bank from Sedan to Verdun. The river formed a natural defensive barrier that would have to be breached.

Rain fell that morning with the same deadening, soaking, chilling cold of six days past. It varied only in intensity, coming at times in lashing sheets of storm hurled by November winds.

The trampled leaves and loam beneath our feet turned to mud. The leafless branches overhead reached starkly at a sodden, rolling sky. In all the world, there wasn't much warmth or peace or comfort. Men knelt against the trunks of trees and slept, using the bulk of log for shelter from the cutting wind. You saw their bearded cheeks close-pressed against the bark. You watched them come awake when shells crashed nearby, the creases in their faces looking like fresh scars.

Losses had been heavy. Some were due to battle—wounds and death—but most were caused by sickness, dysentery and flu. Men, weakened, sought a place of fancied shelter in the brush. They sometimes wrapped a sodden blanket around them and slept. And in sleeping, they died. Exposure, hunger, and sickness took a toll in other ways. One fellow used a bullet on himself and found relief.

Such men as lived with any thought of discipline talked low among themselves or, with still-eyed patience, watched the officers and runners come and go.

"Red" Van Galder slept, full-sprawled beneath a ragged shelterhalf. His helmet made a little tent above his face. Somewhere in the brush, McGuire and Woody Wilson were on call, ready as always for a job to do.

Harris hugged Baldwin's Browning close beneath his blanket, looked in stoic bitterness at everything—and thought of Baldy.

Coxey—the adjutant, a rough and rugged officer—was everywhere about the place, in voice and strength, as though he didn't know what hardship meant.[1] He was the sort of officer soldiers follow anywhere.

---

1. Captain George R. Coxe.

The major snatched a bit of rest inside a little tent.

The fighting waves were but scattered units now. They slogged along through knee-deep mud on what the maps called roads. They passed our place in little ragged columns, plodding doggedly.

A hidden shell hole lurked beneath the slime of mud near where we rested. The plodding men, drunk weary, stumbled into it from time to time and gave us fun. One lanky fellow stepped squarely in the middle of it and landed on the surface with a flop, just saving his face from being ducked by reaching desperately, stiff-armed, beneath the surface. We watched, amused, waiting to hear him curse.

He came up, standing thigh deep in the hole and glanced around to note his audience, threw back his head and roared with laughter. Men who hadn't laughed for days laughed with him.

The laughter spread. It rolled across the rain-soaked woods. It drowned the sound of distant guns. Men laughed 'til tears rolled down through dirty whiskers, joyously, and some slapped strangers on the back in ecstasy.

What a strange spectacle. A little band of men. They knew the fellowship of mud and blood and rain. They knew the fellowship of laughter, miles from home.

"Haven't They Killed You Yet?"

November seventh in the upper Argonne. Behind us lay our last big drive and seven days of war. There were new faces. Men had come and gone. We had known fighting.

I was feeling lonely. Seeking shelter from the cold rain, I leaned against the trunk of a small oak within a short distance of a pup tent occupied by Major Hamilton, our battalion commander. As sergeant of runners, I was on watch to call up a runner should one be needed.

A figure came down the leaf-strewn trail, walking slowly, lacking something of the snap and vigor one expected in a normal man. His head was down, close-ducked against the rain. Something about his lanky, slim-hipped figure rang a little bell of memory of someone known, lost, half-remembered, back along the trail. Coming nearer, I was amazed and happy at the realization of the impossible. My skipper had come back.[1] Weak, wan, haggard, he had been carried out just thirty days before, wounded three times and due for a long vacation. Yet here he was in the upper Argonne woods, seeking out his old command.

I met him with more than the military observance of officer and enlisted man. We met as a skipper and one of his boys. Between us, grooved in memory, lay months of hell and slaughter. Each knew the other's mind, but this was the

---

1. Captain Frank Whitehead.

249

Marine Corps. He was a captain; I was a soldier. I gave him a sharp salute, though much was in my eyes. Here he was again, casual, careless, unassuming, and only the grip of his hand to say how glad he was to come back to his own.

He brushed aside the formality of military training to say, "How in hell are you, Slim? Haven't they killed you yet?"

"Come On, Marines!"

They lied to us that night.[1] Some were bitter at the thought of it. Was this the confidence we'd earned along the road from June? It may have been because we had so many men who still had hope of living. Some of us were not long on the front.

It was a patent, flimsy lie. Old hands among us knew the difference at once and were prepared for anything.

"We're to move a lot of ammunition over to the 89th, to the right of us"—or so the story ran.

There was also talk of Armistice on the morrow.

The fellows didn't really want to fight again—not all of them. We moved away in single file in groping columns, silently, forbidden talk and any extra noise.

Our guns built up a chorus of barrage. We took a winding, downward sort of path among the lesser growth. Someone on the line of march said, "River."

We were going over.[2] The German army held the far bank, as all well knew. Some of us remembered night attacks in other places. One heard men curse our own barrage at such a time because it spoiled the chances of surprise.

---

1. 10–11 November 1918.
2. The river crossing described here and in subsequent chapters was conducted by two battalions of the 5th Marines operating in the 89th Division sector. A similar assault crossing was planned for four marine battalions in the 2d Division sector, but that operation was canceled because constant artillery fire kept the engineers from completing the pontoon bridges.

German gunfire came to meet us. Most of it was high-explosive stuff, thrown blindly anywhere along the little trails we used for our advance. It opened gaps in marching files of men too closely bunched because of forest darkness.

Dead and wounded lay along the paths. No one took the time to care for them. We entered a ravine and scrambled down its rocky, twisting bed below the shelter of its steep-cut walls and had a little space of cover from the shells. Lower toward the river, we walked into a bank of fog. It was like stepping into another world, a much quieter one.

There was a tendency among the men to loiter there in the shelter of the gully slopes. The movement of our little column slowed perceptibly and noncoms cursed and raved quite desperately, trying to keep the men in motion, downward through the night.

Death lashed and tore at the mouth of the ravine, along a railroad track—the general's railroad. Men took deep breaths to fortify themselves before walking into hell.

Running figures scrambled upward past us, frantically endeavoring to fight their way out of that river pit of flame and fog.

The adjutant captured one and pistol-whipped him when he fought to get away. They questioned him, harsh, screaming voices pitched against a roar of sound, machine-gun made, but full of cannon fire, too.

"The bridge, the bridge. Where is the bridge? Come on, guide us—"

We moved off to our right along the track, an automatic jammed tight against the fellow's spine, leading us. Then Coxey stumbled on a broken rail. The guide leaped once or twice against the fog and disappeared. We heard the major curse as he fired, missing him.

A frantic officer of engineers came down the track, arms spread and waving, greeting us profanely, glad to find us. He turned away, pointing as he went, trying to help the major understand the crossing preparations.

Maxims on the far bank of the river found us in the fog and thinned our ranks a bit before they swung away, still firing blindly, anywhere. We lost the officer who had been guiding us, so we kept moving down the track.

We came to some living guide posts along the right of way, our engineers, spaced yards apart along the road we had to take. We heard them faintly, saw them outlined against the flares, and followed them.

We heard them scream, "The bridge! The bridge! This way, come on, marines!"

We saw men totter suddenly against the light and fall as bullets found them; saw other fellows take their places, instantly. "The bridge! Come on! This way!"

We dropped below the rails along the edge of the river and halted where a knot of men were grouped. A rope or two reached forward into the fog. Men clung to them.

We waited for our column to close up, sprawling on the muddy shore, peering at a wall of river mist and fearsome noises.

The Bridge

A man came walking on the water, splashing out of the mist. One heard the swish and fall of timbers underfoot and saw a length of rope, knee high, for use as a guide line.

An officer checked with the man who came across the stream. We who lay nearby caught words that told us many things.

"All set and tied—"

"—maybe a patrol—"

We common soldiers got what dope we could from the engineers who lay among us. We shouted in each other's ears against the noise.

"We built it out of lumber, little rafts, joined end to end—"

"We built it up along the shore, from here—against the current—"

"Cut the top end loose an' that current floated it across—"

"One fellow rode it over, on the end section—"

That was a picture of soldiering, the kind we fellows didn't know, even with all our memories of other places.

A lonely fellow floating into fog, kneeling on a bit of buoyant stuff, knees wet, nervously gripping a rifle.

Did he rest his face along the barrel to gather confidence? Would he find a place to tie off the end of the bridge? Was an enemy patrol waiting for him? Did he shiver in the damp November cold? Armistice, tomorrow . . .

Silly thought, that last. Here's the loom of bank and trees. Hope this rope will reach. I hope—

The major came afoot, still talking hurriedly. Seeing him, the fellows scrambled up. Enough of waiting.

254

The major blew a single, shortened blast and stepped forward, placing one foot on the floating stuff. He never sent a fellow where he wouldn't go himself.

Was it Brents, of Chattanooga, who shouldered him aside? Or was it Red Van Galder? Whoever, the major sprawled in the mud, suddenly off balance.

A dozen fellows hit the bridge with running stride, went splashing on each other's heels. The sections sank knee deep beneath the load while engineers in quick alarm yelled to take wider intervals and tried to stem the tide of men.

Coxey tried to yank a fellow out of line to get his own footing on the bridge. They grappled viciously and tumbled in the mud.

The major, Coxey, and others found a place in line, while the leading figures melted forward into fog—marching single-file in the water toward the guns.

Prayer

The fog was full of flashes, noise, and splashings. Losing contact with the shore, you were abruptly in another world; a world of misty shadows, insecure, unfirm. You walked with little feeling steps toward oblivion.

The floating stuff sank underfoot a bit and left you groping through an inch or two of water. At section ends your weight bore you down until you felt the wash about your ankles and stepped out hurriedly to regain your balance on the next raft. Only the guide ropes beside your knee gave confidence.

Shells crashed in smothered flashes, tearing into the river, sending little waves that washed across your knees. Machine guns yammered in the void, freezing your blood in terror. There was no turning back. Ahead lay everything that was to be.

The mist was thinner in the middle of the stream. It lacked the smoke that hovered near the shadow of the bank. You caught a glimpse of ghostly figures out ahead and slowed to keep a space between yourself and the fellow next in line.

You sensed the shore below the looming shoulders of the hills and felt a little instant urge of hope to tread on earth again. But your hope was drowned in terror as a shell sent waves against the bridge, staggering you.

A stream of Maxim bullets churned up and down the river, searching. They rapped from time to time across the planks, sounding like a sudden roll of muffled drums. You felt their jarring shake all up your limbs and fought against the cramp of belly muscles knotted with fear. You watched men die ahead of you. The second man ahead met the bullets as he stepped across a length of raft, sank to his knees, twisting, and slid face first into the river, vanishing quietly. He left an empty place against the fog.

The next in line half-paused and stepped away as though he gambled on the gun in its brief arc. It was the only chance he had to live.

The bullets ripped a seam along the water, then swung back. They changed their tone abruptly to the *sock, sock, sock* sound bullets make when they hit flesh.

He staggered, held erect by unseen hammers driving him sideways, riveting his body. The guide rope clung a bit across his knees. He fell across it backward, overboard.

The next man stopped in frozen terror before that steep-pitched arc of fire from off the hill. The guide rope led away into the fog. Leaping, twisting water writhed in a hail of fire short yards ahead. In all the world, there was no other path.

He bucked up shaking knees that sagged in awful fear, and fought to keep erect—a man. He stepped forward, then hesitated, stopped, and held a strangled breath.

The night belonged to bitter men who didn't seem to care, who long before had known there was no hope. Because of that, they thought they had conquered fear. The night belonged to fellows late in hell because of memories, and he was one of them in fellowship. The night belonged to him. He was afraid.

Something out of boyhood, something from a little country church came back in a sudden rush, without command, and gave him strength. He spoke out once. "Oh, God!" Two words, a prayer. He moved toward a place of bullet-streaming death. The instant of it left a sense of guilt. He hadn't ever meant to pray again. Prayer was for men who carried faith, and most of them had died in other places.

The Maxims swung away to let him live.

Marooned

Built a bit too long, the bridge had jack-knifed against the far shore. A section slanted upstream, elbow-wise, and left a waist-deep gap of water, frightening the men who walked off into it. Their instant fear of drowning gave way to relief when they felt mud beneath their feet. They hurled themselves against a pitch of breast-high bank, climbed into a little marshy meadow, and waited there.

It was an eerie, ghostly, deadly sort of place, a saucer-shaped hollow hemmed about by brooding wooded hills, a pocket where the shadows hid in fog. Marsh grass was underfoot, bunchy stuff that grew heavy, like roadside clumps of rank timothy. The withered leafy stems were cushions for the sounds we made.

Back of us, the shells and bullets thrashed the river. We stood about in sanctuary for a time, behind the shelter of the storm of fire our enemy laid down to bar our crossing.

We formed a curved defense around the landing place and stepped out carefully into the dark, making room along our little skirmish line for men who joined us from the bridge.

We heard a crashing, filled with cries come off the river, and knew a moment filled with dread when word came down our line, "The bridge is gone!" Not all the shells out there had gone astray. Men knew a little time of almost panic then, realizing we were all alone among the enemy, cut off from reinforcements. Word was passed. "Lie down!" We lay in a semicircle on the bunchy grass; felt knees and elbows sink in mud among the little rain-washed channels through the roots, awaiting orders.

A thousand yards or less away, the tops of hills were lit by dancing fireflies where the enemy gave voice in flame and flash. The gunfire passed above us, riverward, or swept the engineers along the far shore, whence we had come.

The plan of attack was good enough—if it had worked. But the German guns had spoiled the whole of it, and time was passing.

Under the cover of our barrage, the idea had been to rush a storm of bayonet-wielding men rapidly across the river to assault the ring of hills above the landing. Those hills, in our possession, would give us a firing line to base our drive upon.

Infantry, on bridges to the hollow, could follow us and form behind our line, then move off from there. But now we were marooned. We were a lost and desperate band of men, cut off from our battalion and its support. There were a hundred of us, more or less, not nearly enough to take the ring of hills, yet we had to leave the trap of that small vale.

We had advantages: leaders we had followed many times before and fog that blanketed our movements and stifled our noise. The old Boche didn't know we were there. He didn't even send patrols to see. He was content with what his guns had done, were doing, so splendidly.

Desperate expedient. The only open way for fighting men who lived by discipline.

We turned in single line against the rise of ground along the river, heading for the wooded crest that loomed above. The stream was our right flank; our left was fog and nothingness. We walked up quietly to meet the trees.

A rutted, grassy trace of road, the sort a farm cart makes when hauling hay, ran just below the crest in underbrush, along the edge of woods. The forest side of the road was cut against a line of larger trees. It formed a half-high breastwork in the shadow, screened by brush along the open meadowside.

Men met us there, rising from the ground in quick surprise and greeting us with guttural questionings before they died. A few went crashing, running through the trees to sound the alarm. We made the place our own while waiting for day.

The major knelt in the road. Men built a solid tent of blankets over him to shield his flashlight from betraying us. He wrote a message on his pad beneath the pile and struggled up against the weight of stuff that smothered him. He drew a gusty breath of great relief.

A runner went away, alone, to take the message to the far shore; to swim a shell-lashed stream of gruesome things and win a decoration for his act.

Van Galder put our listening posts among the trees, to give us warning if an attack should come. Word of us got to the enemy, who laid a box barrage around our place and on us. He followed up with infantry a time or two, but these laid back to form a line around us in the darkness of the trees, content only to exchange shots. We had to bring our listening posts back in; it was too dangerous to risk the loss of men in the crossfire.

They battered our position with heavy guns, slamming in shells that brought trees down around our ears. We lost old friends who had come with us a long and dreadful way.

Woody Wilson, sprawled high along the shoulder of the bank and looking down a sight along a line of bayonet, made a spectacle against the light of flares. A pudgy, fattish fellow, looking grim, if one can picture it. He always was a joking, jolly sort of cuss; looking tough was difficult for him. No one ever doubted his courage.

He had a place in tales of Belleau Wood and all the other bitter spots along our trail; professed a fear that no one ever saw in dirty places.

A shell fragment broke his leg above the knee and cost him a lot of blood before we got it bandaged.

Woody, pillowed on a blanket in the ditch, grinning and kidding in the glow of Very lights at men who loved him.

Shells brought names and numbers down that night. They killed off men who had a hope of Armistice—tomorrow.

Woody, screaming from another piece of shell, tried desperately to talk to us against the pain. "Dear Soldier Blacksheep."

McGuire ranged up and down the road in bitter, daring

courage, cursing everything in the wholesome, perfect words of a college man.

Andy, who had run away from battle once, in fear. He came back and asked the skipper for another chance. He lay in lanky length among the brush and looked at stars he'd never see again.

The skipper, out of Massachusetts, was talking quietly behind his beak of Yankee nose, from blade-thin lips, to men who needed courage.

Brents of Chattanooga, talking softly in your ear with a Tennessee drawl, low-pitched, unhurried, competent.

Kearns of South Dakota, with a Browning automatic in his hands, waited for movement among the trees.[1]

"Nelly" Messnelli, a hospital corpsman in an army uniform far from his own navy, won a DSC that night while bandaging marines.[2]

D'Armand had a bullet through his heel.

So many died that night, short hours away from Armistice. They had held on to hope in spite of everything. We sensed a thinning grayness in the fog and braced ourselves against the ring of enemies around us. We knew their attack would come with morning.

Gunfire fell away in volume. Machine guns quieted. We heard movements in the wood that fronted us and pictured infantry with bayonets poised to cut down our little band of fellows. We moved our wounded out among the underbrush along the meadow, away from being underfoot when action came.

---

1. Private Andrew A. Kearns.
2. Pharmacist Mate 2d Class Ray A. Messnelli, Distinguished Service Cross, Navy Cross, Silver Star citation, croix de guerre.

We heard a hooting from the hollow where our bridge had been and knew that help had got across. We said a cursing word or two of thanks for the engineers who never quit.

McGuire went scouting in the woods in front of us and found the old Boche gone.

Men dropped and slept almost instantly, worn out with fear and strain.

Dawn of Armistice Day

A battalion from the 89th Division had crossed on one of the five bridges our engineers had built that night in all that storm of shell and bullets. Shells had cut two bridges before they swung across to reach our shore. Men had died on each of them trying to bring help to us.

Stretcher bearers took our wounded to the river. We straightened up our line along the fringe of empty woods. We advanced through little wispy clouds of fog that thinned before our eyes. Figures flitted off ahead among the trees, without resistance, watching us and keeping distance.

A single German gun ahead of us kept throwing shots from time to time among the trees. Repeatedly, the shells kept pace with us. They burst at steady intervals behind our line of men, exploding harmlessly, and followed us the entire width of the woods.

A runner, out of breath with eagerness and news, came shouting from the rear. We heard quick words of questioning and answers.

"Stop where we are?"

"Yes, Armistice—at eleven o'clock. Just wait for orders here—"

"The colonel says—"

We took up line along a grassy drainage ditch above a little valley full of smoke. Men dropped behind rifle barrels that continued to point forward. Bristly, dirty faces pillowed wearily against the feel of weapons, laid in readiness. A row of bayonets kept watch along the front while the men who held the stocks of rifles slept.

263

The Guns Were Still

Rifles lay in readiness atop the little mounds of earth; a row of firing pits, a battle line. The bayonets, like sentinels, winked dully now and then, reflecting the light of distant fires along the front. Machine guns stood out starkly, tripods braced, muzzles peering ahead like eager, watchful dogs against the dark.

The men were restless, wakeful, gathering about in little groups on blankets spread against the damp. They talked in quiet tones among themselves.

Habit hid their cigarets against their breasts, still fearful that an enemy would spot the glow. Lone fellows took their ease in quiet, staring thoughtfulness. Why did they, like their bayonets, peer toward the front? Was something gone? Why did no single one of them look toward the rear?

There was a nervous tension in the air. It shattered when a fellow struck a match or laughed or raised his voice or moved too suddenly.

At such time one saw men's heads snap up in quick alarm, in instant, wary watchfulness, and saw them search the shadows near at hand, then heard the hearty breath of quick relief as they remembered, trying to talk in a normal tone of voice, like normal men.

Was there ever in the history of our race a night like that? So queer, so still, so full of listening?

Silence laid a pall on everything that first night after the Armistice. The guns of four long years were still at last.